AF649207

The Family History Book

Cassie Gilmartin has 20 years of experience in writing and editing family history, including eight years as the publisher and editor of the award-winning magazine *Inside History*. She is co-host and producer of the *Portrait Detective* podcast in collaboration with Margot Riley from the State Library of New South Wales. Cassie's fascination with family history started when her mum told her she was descended from an Irish highwayman and a madam of a brothel, of the Lower Sort.

Shaun Gilmartin has specialised in history and science programming as a TV executive producer and writer for more than two decades, working for broadcasters across the globe. His documentaries have won awards in the UK, the US and Europe. It has taken him all these years to discover more about his father, who died when he was just two.

'Now your frequent cry, "I'd write the family history if I knew where to start", is silenced. This book is so rich in example and so charming that it will not only tell you exactly where to start and proceed but will also entertain and enthuse you. Your descendants in 2524 are crying for you to follow this guide and leave them a history that makes their forebears enchanting.'

Tom Keneally

'An invaluable resource. This is a book guaranteed to inspire, educate and support experienced and budding family historians alike. It's gloriously user-friendly – not least because the Gilmartins are so friendly – not only keeping up with all the modern trends in digital research, but also staying true to the timeless, compulsive motivations of family history: curiosity, creativity and love.'

Clare Wright

'An extraordinarily helpful guide – up to date on techniques and sources that simply weren't available a decade ago. Cassie and Shaun are lively and reliable guides to an absorbing and popular historical endeavour that can so easily trick and mislead the unwary.'

Peter Stanley

'A very accessible guide on how to get started – and keep going – with your family history.'

Brad Argent, Ancestry Studios

'An exceptional level of detail on the records and sources for each chapter. Cassie and Shaun should be congratulated on an excellent work.'

Ruth Graham, Society of Australian Genealogists

The Family History Book

How to trace your ancestors in Australia

CASSIE GILMARTIN
& SHAUN GILMARTIN

NEWSOUTH

UNSW Press acknowledges the Bedegal people, the Traditional Owners of the unceded territory on which the Randwick and Kensington campuses of UNSW are situated, and recognises the continuing connection to Country and culture. We pay our respects to Bedegal Elders past and present.

A NewSouth book

Published by
NewSouth Publishing
University of New South Wales Press Ltd
University of New South Wales
Sydney NSW 2052
AUSTRALIA
https://unsw.press/

© Cassie Gilmartin and Shaun Gilmartin 2024

10 9 8 7 6 5 4 3 2 1

This book is copyright. Apart from any fair dealing for the purpose of private study, research, criticism or review, as permitted under the Copyright Act, no part of this book may be reproduced by any process without written permission. Inquiries should be addressed to the publisher.

NATIONAL LIBRARY OF AUSTRALIA

A catalogue record for this book is available from the National Library of Australia

ISBN 9781742237824 (paperback)
9781742239101 (ebook)
9781761178078 (ePDF)

Internal design Josephine Pajor-Markus
Cover design Lisa White
Cover images Cassie Gilmartin's maternal grandparents on their engagement day, 1940. Background photos by Nana studio/Shutterstock (front) and ADragan/Shutterstock (back)
Printed and bound by CPI Group (UK) Ltd, Croydon, CR0 4YY

All reasonable efforts were taken to obtain permission to use copyright material reproduced in this book, but in some cases copyright could not be traced. The authors welcome information in this regard.

This book is printed on paper using fibre supplied from plantation or sustainably managed forests.

UNSW SYDNEY

Dedicated to our families in Australia,
the UK and South Africa.

The authors acknowledge Australia's Aboriginal and Torres Strait Islander peoples as the Traditional Custodians of the land on which we work and live, and give respect to the Elders past and present.

First Nations readers are advised that chapter 7 contains the name of someone who has died.

Contents

A note from the authors

Hello family historians, we're so glad you're here.

First up, allow us to introduce ourselves. We're a husband and wife team who met through our love of history. One of us (Cassie) was the publisher of *Inside History*, a print and digital media brand that showcased family history research and the stories it reveals. The other (Shaun) was a television executive producer working on history programs in Australia and the UK. We arrived at the topic of family history through different paths, but with the same enthusiasm and respect for this worthwhile endeavour. Below, we've each written a bit more about ourselves individually, including what we've discovered when we researched our family histories.

CASSIE I caught the family history bug as a 20-something when my mum, Barbara Hall, herself a family historian, told me that I was descended from an Irish highwayman and a madam of a Dublin brothel, of the 'Lower Sort'. This revelation supercharged my interest. It made me want to understand who they were and what their lives were like, both in Ireland and in the colony of New South Wales.

Barbara decided to research the 1000-plus Irish convicts who arrived directly from Ireland between 1791 and 1800. The reason? To put the lives and experience of that highwayman, Edward Turley Smith, and the madam, Jane Maher, who arrived in 1796 and 1797 respectively, into context. (You'll see Edward and Jane featured here and there in this book.) This research became a series of six books, each detailing one of the six convict ships to arrive during those years – in chronological order these ships were the *Queen* (1791); *Boddingtons* (1793); *Sugar Cane* (1793); *Marquis Cornwallis* (1796); *Britannia* (1797) and *Minerva* (1800). Each book contained biographies on every convict and soldier on board, from their crimes and trials in Ireland to their lives in New South Wales (see our section on further resources for details). I edited those books and became thoroughly involved and interested in the convicts. How could I not? There was Daniel Fane, the Burning Boy from County Limerick; Mr Knaresbro, gentleman convict and seducer of heiresses; George Massey, convicted robber of the Bank of Ireland; Ann Grant, a small-time thief in Dublin who became a successful shopkeeper in Sydney's Pitt Street; Mary Bryan, Mary Curren and Catherine McLean, highwaywomen who dressed as men to rob the Wicklow mail coach; James Don Butler, alias Captain Fearnought; and many many more.

But looking back, my fascination started even earlier when, as a nine-year-old, I accompanied Barbara to the Mitchell Library in Sydney one day. We were there to access some microfilm (it was a long time ago – nothing was digital back then) to look for records for my great-grandmother Kezia Readford. We found one, except that in the record her name was spelt Cassia – similar to my own name. That's when I felt the power of connection through the records. I couldn't have put my reaction into words as a child, but to this day I clearly remember that moment.

That's the reason – it seems to me – that we resonate with our family history. We are who we are because of our ancestors. These records, whether in paper form, or via stories handed down through generations, reach out through the decades and centuries that separate us and them, and connect us.

Over the years I've given many seminars and talks on how to research your family history. And at those I always say, 'Everyone loves history; they just don't know they do'. Think of the biggest television series over the past decade or so. *Downton Abbey. Peaky Blinders. Vikings.* All based on history. So many of us have a fascination with the past. We want to know where we came from. But a lot of the time, it seems too overwhelming, and too time-consuming, to trawl through records, whether digital or on paper, tracing the family tree. But if you follow a few simple guidelines to set you on the right path, you'll find it uncovers more than you'd ever thought possible.

SHAUN Unlike Cassie, I was infected by the family history bug later in life – in my 30s, to be precise. Up until then, history meant 'world history' – the fall of the apartheid regime in South Africa, the smashing down of the wall in Berlin signalling the end of the Soviet Era, the Good Friday agreement that allowed the warring factions in Northern Ireland to form government together. I had documented these events, amongst numerous others, first as a video journalist then as a TV documentary producer. I was lucky enough to be covering the stories that would become the texts of future history tomes.

It was not until my mother, after much persuasion, gave me a photograph of a man she said was my father that I realised I had been ignoring a black hole in my personal life.

I never knew my dad – he died when I was just two. As I stared at the photo, a middle-aged man, pipe in hand, standing jauntily with one leg on the bumper of his car, stared back at me. It was an eerie moment. I feel the goose bumps on my skin now as I recall it. Half of my DNA came from this man, yet I knew nothing about him.

And so began a trawl through records of every kind to fill in the blanks in my early history that a reticent mother was unwilling to divulge. Armed only with his name and a guesstimate of his date of birth, I have been able to unearth all manner of detail – including a document with an astonishing revelation.

During my career as a documentary maker I have flown in all sorts of aircraft – from passenger airliners to RAF squadrons. My filming with the latter included missions over war zones. The document I found in the National Archives in the UK had an uncanny pre-echo: my father had been an RAF pilot in the First World War, flying missions over war-torn Europe. Was this why I felt so at home in the air? Had his wartime experience made its way to me through his genes? Whatever the answer, discovering I had that strong connection with my father was a pivotal moment in my research.

*

We want to share with you our passion for family history. We enjoy the process of understanding more about our own families' pasts; it is fascinating and rewarding in equal measure. Whether you are beginning with just one piece of your past or you already have a tonne of information to wade through, we will give you the starting tools, tips and tricks to uncover your ancestry – you never know what you might discover. These discoveries can be joyous, confronting, enriching and frustrating.

The purpose of this book is to encourage you to start researching your family tree in Australia, beginning with the present (you) and going back as far as you can in the records. Perhaps you have already got going, but stopped due to not knowing where to go next. This book is for beginners who want to make that start, and for those who've started but put it aside and now want to re-engage.

We feel it's important to frame the context of this book. The records that we refer to are colonial in origin, accessed via government and private archives, libraries and press reports. By and large these records are paper-based – birth, death and marriage records, passenger lists, convict indents, military attestations – but you'll also find other formats, such as photographs and audio recordings. Then there are personal archives that you may have – photographs, ephemera and oral histories handed down. Some family history in the context of Australia is relatively recent, from the post-war eras; others go back for millennia. In this book we have covered records that pertain to instances where ancestors interacted with the government authorities, both in the colonial period and post-Federation in 1901. These are documents we have easy access to – many have been digitised and are readily available.

As family historians, the records we look at reflect the attitudes, laws and language of the time. Some include terms and views that are not appropriate today. These can be confronting and distressing, especially when they raise issues of racism, sexism and xenophobia. This is particularly relevant for those researching Indigenous ancestors. These records reflect the period in which they were created and do not coalesce with our views. To bring these things to light through family history research hopefully means that we can understand the past, and move forward to a better and fairer future.

Each chapter is focused on a collection of records that relate to each other and covers records and databases that are indispensable for finding your family tree, from birth, marriage and death certificates and convict records, to newspapers and military records. We also cover the more recent appetite for DNA tests – what they are, what they mean and what they can reveal. By focusing each chapter on a collection of records, the book is designed to be dipped in and out of. Within most chapters you'll find a summary of common terms to familiarise yourself with, and at the end of the book, there is a list of resources to further help you research your family in Australia.

You'll see that for each chapter we've interviewed family history experts from across the nation so that you can hear directly from them. People with decades of experience who are willing to share all that they've learned while working in the field. Because if you do start your family history, you'll soon discover it's all about collaboration – sharing knowledge, discoveries, triumphs and frustrations. When you have a Eureka moment – when you find something you've been searching for, that elusive 'aha' moment – it's your fellow family historians who will understand your euphoria and satisfaction. They'll also understand just how addictive family history can be, once it gets its hooks into you.

Throughout this book you'll see words and phrases such as 'most likely', 'may appear', 'can sometimes indicate' and so on. The only thing we can say with surety is that there will be anomalies in the records! This book is designed to get you started, rather than provide an exhaustive list of each and every record relating to a topic. Our thoughts are based on our own experience and from talking to a lot of experienced people in the industry, many of whom we feature in this book. Sometimes in family history, the record will not exist, or the record exists but your ancestor's name does not appear because perhaps there are pages missing, or the records keeper at the time didn't include your ancestor's details. Or you're tracing a female ancestor and unless she was a career criminal or a socialite, she may *never* appear in records, other than within a birth, marriage or death notice. Those with some experience are nodding as they read this. It happens, and it's frustrating.

Case in point: Cassie's ancestor appeared on charges of fraud against the government in 1802. The historical document detailing the case goes on for three pages, listing witnesses against the defendant, and what they said. But the fourth page, which would have contained the verdict of the case, is *missing*. Probably (there's another one of those non-committal words) never to be found. Cue immense frustration! All you can do is keep good records of what you do find, read widely about the era you're researching to give you context, and make logical conclusions based on the evidence you do have by cross-checking everything. And remember, new records are coming online all the time, so it's worth looking at online databases again if it's been a while between checks.

The good news is that you will probably find an enormous amount of information. We're on this journey with you – we're here to inspire and to give you a head start. The rest is up to you. But we promise, we really promise, that it'll be worth it!

So with this in mind, let's dive straight in.

Cassie and Shaun

Golden rules of family history

There are a few guidelines to follow when starting your family history research. Here are the ones we feel are most beneficial.

1 Work backwards. Start with yourself. Put your birth certificate in a file with some information about you, where you've lived, your occupation and so on. Then do the same with your parents and grandparents.
2 Talk to family members and record everything they tell you, even if that's just 'Nonna lived in Kogarah, New South Wales, in the 1950s'. Anything you can verify will help to build up a picture of your ancestors' lives.
3 Set achievable goals and have a research plan. Research one branch at a time and decide what information you're looking for at the outset.
4 Cite your sources. Keep an accurate record of where, when and what you've found for each person. You never know when you'll need to refer back to your primary source, and it's maddening when you can't find it – or you can't refer someone to it – because you didn't notate it correctly.
5 Cross-reference everything. Don't assume someone else's information is accurate: do your own research. Try and get at least two sources for the same piece of information. Create a timeline in your ancestor's life so you can see where they were at any given time. This will help you spot any irregularities in the dates on the records.

6 Always try spelling variations for first and last names when searching a data set. Spellings of people's names will vary across sources. Cassie's highwayman ancestor appears under several monickers in the records – as Turley-Smith, Turley, Smith, Thurley, Thurlough. Gilmartin can just as easily appear somewhere as Kilmartin. Think logically yet broadly when searching the records.

7 Look at the entire page of the record. Later convict indents, for example, have information on both the left and right pages. The left gives you their name, age, marital status, children, trade and trial details, while the right has details of their term of sentence, any former convictions, height, physical appearance and notes from their time in the colony.

8 Make sure the record set that you're about to search is within the relevant date range. Check what records it contains and from when. Records will span a certain period; for example, death records in a particular collection might end in 1912, which isn't of any use if you're searching for an ancestor who died in 1925.

9 Allow some quality time for research, because family history is utterly absorbing and addictive. We were looking at First World War diaries in our research for this book, found one online and ended up reading it for two hours. The soldier wasn't related to us; it was just so interesting reading his thoughts as he prepared to be sent to the Front. No time is ever wasted. Everything you read and research adds to the picture you have of the times in which your ancestors lived.

10 Enjoy the process of discovery – this is all about you!

CHAPTER 1

How to start in three easy steps

AT A GLANCE: *Researching your family history can be overwhelming. So we'll break it down into three easy steps to help you get going.*

1 ***Start with what you know***

The secret to starting a family history? Start with the present and work backwards. We'll show you what this means.

2 ***Talk to family members***

We'll discuss how to become an interviewer, and what to ask family members to discover more about your family tree.

3 ***Define your goals***

There is a bewildering amount of information out there and if you don't have definitive goals to frame your research, then it's very easy to be put off and give up. We will discuss what sort of goals to aim for and how to make them accessible so that you keep going and find out more about your ancestors.

COMMON TERMS YOU'LL COME ACROSS

Ancestor These are the people who lived before you. The term usually refers to anyone born before your grandparents. Ancestors also include those who are not directly from the same line, such as aunts, uncles and cousins.

Antecedent The people before you, including your parents and grandparents. You are a descendant of your parents, while your parents are your antecedents.

Bachelor A man who has never been married.

Descendant Someone who comes after a particular ancestor. Children, grandchildren and so on are descendants.

Family tree vs pedigree chart A family tree lists your direct ancestors as well as indirect ancestors such as aunts, uncles and cousins. A pedigree chart lists only your direct family – parents, grandparents, great-grandparents and so on.

Genealogy A line of descent that can be traced continuously from an ancestor. The terms 'genealogy' and 'family history' are used interchangeably, but genealogy is the more technical term, referring to the process of research and sources to document a family history.

Maiden or birth name The surname a woman is born with.

Maternal line The line of ancestry that follows from your mother's side.

Paternal line The line of ancestry that follows from your father's side.

Spinster An unmarried woman, often someone older who is considered unlikely to marry.

> I always ask the celebrity at the outset to have an open mind and an open heart. Because we never know what we'll uncover in our research.
>
> Maxine Gray, executive producer, *Who Do You Think You Are?* Australia

Chances are you're reading this because you're curious. Curious about who you are, and about those who came before you. Curious about what sort of lives they led, and how that's influenced yours – not only from a genetic point of view, but their life experiences and the decisions they made. This is, after all, the story of you.

In our introduction we talked about how we fell in love with family history, and why we're encouraging everyone to trace their family tree. But it's not just the satisfaction, and the thrill of hunting for ancestors. There are tangible benefits to researching your family history – here are five of them.

You're preserving your family's history

An obvious reason to start with, of course. But in our experience there's often one person in a family who gets the genealogy bug and becomes the keeper of the family photographs, knows the exact relationship between great-uncle Alfred and cousin Clarence, or says that your handwriting is exactly like Yiayia's. If that's going to be you (or already is you) then be proud. You're allowing your ancestors to live on by documenting their stories. You're building a patchwork of information that will be cherished by future generations.

And remember, you're about to meet family you never knew existed. Because when you're building your family tree, you will no doubt meet extended branches of the family to swap research with. Sometimes these family members are closer than you think, geographically speaking. We kid you not – we've met people who've told us that they started researching their family tree only to find a previously unknown cousin living in the next street. Or the neighbouring suburb. True stories. Family history really is amazing at bringing strangers together.

You'll feel part of a community

There's a real community spirit among family historians. We've seen, and been the recipients of, strangers swapping information and offering advice to smash through brick walls. We've heard people say, 'Oh I live near that cemetery, I'll drop by this week and search for your ancestor's grave'. People are incredibly generous with their time and knowledge, and you'll find yourself reciprocating that. Case in point – all our experts interviewed for this book took time out from their busy schedules to willingly share their research experiences. You'll also understand more about the local and social context of your ancestor's life and the area in which they lived.

You'll become an ace detective

Family history is all about looking for clues that will help you solve a mystery. It could be trying to find where an ancestor is buried, or why someone moved to the other side of the world to marry, leaving their entire family behind. Whatever the circumstances, it's your job to look for the breadcrumbs in the historical records. Family history demands sharp investigative skills, backed up with finding enough evidence to prove (or discard) your theory. It uses logic, computer skills, problem-solving, mathematics and intuition. It'll teach you to double- and even triple-check everything you find. Keep investigating and you'll be as sharp as Hercule Poirot in no time.

Family history can make you smarter

Here's the really cool part. In 2010, research published in the *European Journal of Social Psychology* showed that thinking about our ancestors can boost our performance on intelligence tests. The researchers called this the 'ancestor effect'. They proved their theory by asking undergraduate students to either think about their ancestors for five minutes or think about a recent shopping trip. The groups who thought about their ancestors were more confident afterwards in their abilities to pass exams, and attempted to answer more questions. Three further studies showed that thinking or writing about their recent or distant ancestors led students to actually perform better on a range of intelligence tests, including verbal and spatial tasks.

Their conclusion? That 'normally, our ancestors managed to overcome a multitude of personal and society problems, such as severe illnesses, wars, loss of loved ones or severe economic declines. So, when we think about them, we are reminded that humans who are genetically similar to us can successfully overcome a multitude of problems and adversities'.

It'll get personal

Learning about your ancestors can help you discover more about yourself. After all, it's their blood coursing through your veins.

As we've already mentioned, discovering how our ancestors overcame adversity gives you a stronger sense of identity and resilience. One of Cassie's convict ancestors, the brothel madam Jane Maher, was transported on the *Britannia*, arriving in Sydney in 1797. It was dubbed a 'hell ship' due to the sadistic nature of the ship's captain, who was paranoid about an Irish mutiny occurring during the voyage. He withheld rations from the convicts, wouldn't let them exercise on deck, and had at least one convict flogged to death. Two women committed suicide by jumping overboard. Jane survived that ordeal and went on to start a bakery at the Rocks within a year of her arrival. We like to think her resilience shines right through the generations to the present day.

These are some of the reasons why so many are getting hooked on family history. You may think that researching ancestors who lived 100, 200 or 300 years ago won't really affect you – these people who you've never met, and who are names on a historical record. But when you see their photographs, read their handwriting on a document, and piece together their lives, you'll realise that they don't feel so far away at all.

This last point about things getting personal was mentioned by every expert we interviewed for this book as a particularly important one: researching someone with a strong connection to you can be rewarding, but also confronting. Especially so with Indigenous family history. Melissa Jackson, a librarian at the State Library of New South Wales (SLNSW) and a Bundjalung woman, has been helping people research their Indigenous family history for three decades and has seen this first hand. 'You never know when a record is going to be confronting. For example, I was looking at Aborigines Welfare Board letters that (I thought) my grandfather had written. And so I jokingly looked at them and thought, "Oh, no, that's my grandmother's handwriting". And then it just hit me: *That's my grandmother's handwriting*. And it was about a loan to build a house. They got knocked back in the end, but it really rammed home that my grandfather didn't have an education; that my grandmother had to write these letters. And they had to go cap in hand to the Welfare Board saying can you give us a loan. So inadvertently, you come across these confronting personal records.'

Melissa's advice in this situation is to have family members with you when you are researching or reading a document. 'Don't go alone. If you are strong enough to do that, more power to you, but try and have family members with you so that you can leave the room and go outside. Ground yourself, have a hug, have a cry, that type of thing.

'As a professional – except if it relates to my family, then I'm weepy, I'm just weepy – but as a professional, I try and look beyond the words and look at the substance of the record. So what does that record tell me? The birth, the death, the marriage: if it has words that offend in the record – words such as quadroon or half-caste, those types of quantitative things – I try and look beyond the record. When I do information requests on behalf of other people, I always speak about that. Before I share the record, I always say this record has this type of word or these type of words in there and what we have to focus on is that this tells us a little bit more about the person. Oftentimes it is the innocuous record that will be confronting, so have somebody with you so you can step back. Make sure your cultural safety is okay. Ground yourself and then go back in.'

*

No matter who or what you are looking for, and before you consult any records, start a free trial on Ancestry, or do a DNA test, there are three steps to take to get you on the right path. They're easy to follow, don't cost anything except your time, and don't require any high-tech wizardry know-how.

STEP 1

Start with what you know

The first golden rule when embarking on your family history is to begin with yourself and work backwards. Grab a notebook, or open a new Word doc on your computer. List your name, your date of birth, and if relevant, the date you were married. If you have a copy of your birth and/or marriage certificates, then place them into a folder, either electronically or in physical form.

Now move backwards to your parents and do the same thing. Start by writing or typing key dates in their lives. We would highly recommend you order birth certificates for your parents if you or they don't have a copy somewhere already, and death certificates, if relevant. (We'll talk more about certificates in chapter 4.) Put them in a folder labelled with their name. This sort of methodical documentation will set you up with good habits.

Genealogist Danielle Lautrec knows this all too well. Danielle has years of experience in family history and teaches genealogy courses at the Society of Australian Genealogists. One of her key pieces of advice to students is to gather vital information early on in the research process. 'One of the things that I teach is a principle that I call the solid foundation, which is that you have to have a solid foundation of information before you start doing your research. So your baseline information needs to be accurate with evidence (to back it up) because if your base is not accurate, the rest of your research will be wrong.

'You really literally have to start with yourself. Because a lot of people will start with grandparents or some person they've heard about that they think is really important. But unless you start with yourself and move backwards in time, you're not going to have that solid foundation. So even [though] I started 20 to 30 years ago, it was only in the last few years that I found out my father was adopted. If I had started with my father's birth certificate and looked at it more carefully and understood what it was saying, I might have found that out earlier. You really do have to start right from yourself.'

Grab a blank sheet of paper. Write your name at the top. Don't worry about siblings, aunts, uncles or cousins for this exercise. Draw a line downwards and write in your parents' full names (use your mother's birth name), date of birth, date of marriage, if relevant, and date of death, if relevant. From your mother's name, draw a line downwards again and write her parents' full names (your maternal grandparents) and any key dates that you know for them. Do the same for your father's parents (your paternal grandparents). For most people that's as far back as they can go without consulting records or other members of the family, but if you know any details of your family further back; that is, the parents of your grandparents, keep the exercise going until you've exhausted your knowledge.

Congratulations, you now have the beginnings of your family tree.

There's also a chance that you've come to the topic of family history via watching celebrities learn about their family history on *Who Do You Think You Are?*, the hit series that has been on our TV screens for more than a decade and a half. This first step of starting with what you know is a universal

TOP TIP A family tree that lists you, your parents, your grandparents and so on is called a pedigree chart, because it shows only your direct antecedents. This is a good way to start. As you dig deeper, you can add extended family members, such as aunts, uncles and cousins.

one when it comes to beginning your family history – even the researchers on *Who Do You Think You Are?* approach their research for an episode by first asking the celebrity what they know about their family. Executive producer Maxine Gray says that this is essential to set up the episode and to help decide which research avenue to pursue. 'The first thing I do is set up a Zoom call with the celebrity, or I go and meet them in person. And I ask them, one: what they know; two: what they don't know; and three; what they want to know. And then I ask them about themselves and the questions they have about why they are the way they are and why their parents are the way they are. And those things inform our research.'

STEP 2

Talk to family members

Once you've charted what *you* know, it's time to consult other family members and find out what *they* know about your genealogy. Some people have found a cousin who pops out of the woodwork and says they've done the family history back many generations. That's fabulous and exciting and obviously a big help, but remember, that ingenious cousin is only *one* side of your family and, like all good detectives, you'll still need to check their research to make sure it's accurate.

But for now, let's assume you don't have a cousin with a treasure trove of information, which is what brought you to this book in the first place. Never fear, a whole world of intrigue and detective work awaits you!

When doing these family interviews, you're looking not only for key dates of birth, marriage and death that are missing from the chart you've just made, but also for information that will start fleshing out your family tree: occupations, the suburbs or streets where they lived, the schools they went to. That sort of oral history is invaluable for confirming or disputing information that you'll later discover during your research. As you go further in your family history journey, ideally you'll be looking for three sources of information to confirm if you have the right ancestor, in the right place, at the right time, and stories handed down to you from older members of the family become priceless.

How to interview a family member

Many of us make promises to ourselves that, one day, we'll interview older family members and record their trip down memory lane. It really is an important step into starting your family history journey because it'll set up your research.

> **TOP TIP** If you can, plan to chat with the eldest member of the family – they could give you a wealth of information.

Interviewing an older family member will also help bring those first few branches on your family tree to life. We've met so many family historians who all wish they'd written down the stories their parents or grandparents told them. Because here's the thing: you think you'll remember all those great stories they told you. And the recipes they cooked for you. Or the names of everyone in that very Edwardian photograph hanging on their wall. But you won't. Those details and memories will become sketchy, no matter your age. So we can't encourage you enough to set aside some time to interview those elderly members of your family. And we predict they'll love the experience as well.

SLNSW librarian Melissa Jackson agrees that if you can speak with family, take the opportunity. 'And when you do, quote your sources. So "I spoke with Auntie on this day, and this is what was said". Memories are great, but we all have so many things happening these days. Note the details. Where did you have that yarn? What was the date? Because you'll want to get back to that later.'

Choose the oldest family member who is the closest relative to you. Start by planning when to do the interview – or even a series of short interviews, especially if your family member doesn't have much energy for long conversations. Let them know what you'd like to talk about and, if possible, print out the questions for them beforehand.

Ask for details about their parents and grandparents, such as birth, marriage and death dates and locations; the areas in which they lived (addresses are a bonus as they'll come in handy later); their occupations; and any other big events in their lives. Again, anything you can glean here will set you up later as you start using records to discover more about their lives.

You'll often see this technique in episodes of *Who Do You Think You Are?*, when early on the celebrity will talk to family

TOP TIP Before you interview them, have a sense of the history of their times, and that of their parents and grandparents. They may have been caught up in wars or been part of the Stolen Generation, and so bringing up these stories may be painful. Conversely, they may be delighted that someone is interested to hear their stories.

members about a particular branch of their tree that they're hoping to find more about. This technique is an effective way to hear oral histories. In most cases the family member will have photographs or ephemera such as family letters or a bible to show the celebrity. It's really a tangible way to immediately connect them with their past. As Maxine says, 'It can provoke a deep feeling of connection for a celebrity to hold a letter or a journal that was written 150 years ago. Or even to look at a photograph of a great-grandparent and recognise something in their face that has been handed down through the generations. I'll never forget Todd McKenney being completely mesmerised looking at a really fuzzy and quite degraded photograph of a family member and feeling a really strong connection to that person.'

Make sure you sit somewhere quiet and comfortable so you can record the interview and hear everything that is being said. Have snacks and drinks to hand to keep energy levels up. You don't need a lot of tech – taking a video on your smartphone will do the trick, or using a free dictaphone app. And there is plenty of free editing software out there if you want to get a bit more creative. Just make sure you save everything and create a backup file as well – you won't have a TV crew doing this for you!

INTERVIEW QUESTIONS

We've compiled a list of interview questions for you to consider when chatting with a parent or grandparent, and this list may prompt other ideas for you as well.

- When and where were you born?
- Where did you attend school?
- What was your first job?
- When and where were you married?
- What was the address of your first home?
- What was the house like?
- At what age did you move from that house?
- Where else have you lived and what were the addresses?
- What were your parents' names?
- When and where were they born and married?
- When and where did they pass away?
- What were their occupations?
- What is your earliest memory?
- How would you describe your parents – in looks and personality?
- What are some of the key moments in your life?
- Do you have any certificates or documents I can see?

Ask questions that will encourage your relative/s to start talking and that result in varied answers and stories. And please, please, go through any old photographs, make copies (take a picture on your phone if nothing else) and write down the names of the people in them. Again, you might think you'll remember them down the track, but we guarantee you won't.

TOP TIP AI transcription services are great for transcribing interviews, but they aren't perfect, so go over the transcript after the interview while the details are still fresh in your mind. This way you can correct any of the text, particularly people's names, that has been transcribed incorrectly.

For our expert interviews featured in this book we used our laptop and an AI software program called Otter. Otter's basic features are free, which should suffice for your interview/s. We like Otter because it will record the interview as well as transcribe it for you, which is fantastic when you want to read a transcript to look for key information. However, we recommend you write down any key names in case Otter misspells them, to save you checking back with your relative later on.

What you discuss with your relative/s is entirely up to you. However, as a general rule, we'd suggest you have specific questions in mind, such as 'Where was your mum born?' and 'Do you know where she went to school?' We would encourage you to talk about specific things as well as general memories, so for instance: 'Tell me about your wedding day'. You'll get all sorts of details about their wedding that you won't find anywhere else and will be something that you can add to your family history notes to hand down to others in the family.

STEP 3
Define your goals

Now to our third step. When you're starting out this step is just as important as the first two, in our opinion. This is because family history can very quickly become overwhelming when your goal is to 'research your family tree'. It's such a broad term. Remember, your direct ancestors will double with each generation that you go back. So, you have two parents, four grandparents, eight great-grandparents, 16 great-great-grandparents, and so on. That's a lot of branches – and that's just your direct ancestors – so set your goal early on.

For the researchers at *Who Do You Think You Are?*, their goal is to find a cracking story that will engage the celebrity and the audience, and one which will translate to the screen. 'We look for those things that we think will resonate deep within the celebrity and that will give us an emotional resonance when we get to the end', says Maxine.

And a goal can often come from the celebrity themselves: 'I don't know anything about my father's side of the family', or 'There's a family rumour my grandfather went to jail' can often set up the premise of the episode. As Maxine says, 'It's important to feel that the celebrity is going on a quest. It's always a quest to discover things about their family, but you want it to be something that they or someone in their family has always been curious about. So that's what we look for, because sometimes the celebrity themselves may not have a deep curiosity about any one specific thing but sometimes, for example, it's something their mother has always wanted to know. Perhaps it's a family myth: was it true or not?'

As viewers of the show will know, each episode focuses on one celebrity and the storyline gradually reveals things about their family history, focusing on what they are curious about. 'We like to lay the groundwork in the premise of the episode for the celebrity to uncover information that will shed some light on those particular things', says Maxine. 'For some, it may not be particularly personal – like Barry Humphries discovering a scandal and a brush with royalty. Perfect. That's what you want for Barry Humphries. But then with Troy Cassar-Daly, he said at the beginning of his episode he felt like he grew up in two different worlds: the Indigenous world with his mother, and the Maltese world with his father's family. He is very close to both sides, but as a kid, he had to bridge those worlds and that was so hard for him.'

The episode with the singer-songwriter Troy Cassar-Daly is a great example of the power of the research that the show uncovers, and how it can help you to understand your family. An example of this is when Troy journeys back to Malta, as Maxine explains. 'On the show we took Troy back to Malta, and he went down into the tunnels where his grandmother, his father as a child, and in fact the whole family lived for months, because the Italians bombed the hell out of Malta. That tiny little island was the most bombed place on earth during the Second World War, and to take Troy there was incredible because his father never wanted to go back to Malta. And Troy didn't understand why. But when we took him back, and he heard the stories, and he saw the house where they lived, and he heard how everything, including his parents' house, had been flattened, he said, "Now I understand. My father didn't want to go back because in his mind, there was nothing to go back to". By coming on the show and learning more about both sides of his family, the Maltese and the Indigenous, Troy finally felt more emotionally connected to both those worlds and more at peace.'

And – this may surprise you – don't ignore the family myths, says Maxine. 'What I've learned is that if there's a family myth, there's something there … where there's smoke, there's fire. And it may be that somebody said we had a Spanish grandmother or great-grandmother. Well, actually, it turns

TOP TIP Keep your goals realistic and attainable, and focus on one side of your family at a time. In chapter 3, we'll talk about building a research plan and keeping a research log to help you on your quest.

out, it was an Indigenous great-grandmother. Or that there was a scandal. I think those those little stories that come down through the generations are definitely worth probing. And I think those stories would be great motivators for readers of your book to set out on a quest of their own.'

It's great advice for when you're setting your own goals. Try to keep them contained and defined at first – you don't have a team of expert researchers doing the work for you, so starting small will keep it manageable. Think about what you'd like to discover – and that becomes your first goal, or quest. It could be to discover when your maternal and paternal family arrived in Australia. Perhaps you want to discover if any of your ancestors served in the First World War or if there's a convict in the family closet. Perhaps it's to research back three generations, then take stock and set a new goal.

These things are all possible. Targeting one thing will help you feel like you've accomplished your goals, which will incentivise you to keep going. Just keep your eye on the prize: remember your goal and go for it!

There are two things that Maxine enjoys the most about heading up *Who Do You Think You Are?*. 'The best thing is hearing from the celebrity afterwards, and them saying how much they enjoyed going on the journey, and what a gift it was to them. And the other thing is that I'm exposed to those personal histories, as well as history across different countries, different continents and different periods of time. [The fact] that I can do that work is a gift to me.'

It's clear how much the celebrities enjoy the journey of discovering their family history. We feel that your search will be equally rewarding. Now that you've identified your goals, gleaned what information you can by talking to family members, and seen where the information gaps are, it's time to start hitting those historical records, either online or in person. But before we do, there are some housekeeping things that we need to discuss in the next couple of chapters, such as an introduction to our state and national libraries and archives, what you'll find online, and how to build a family tree chart.

CHAPTER 2

The 'who, what and where' of family history records

AT A GLANCE: *We'll do a quick introductory tour around the country on the key institutions, such as libraries and archives, that have the majority of the records most useful to family history research. We'll also cover the 'big four' subscription sites and what they hold, plus an emerging fifth contender building a biographical database with a difference.*

> 'I will endeavour to get away by stealth the first opportunity.'
>
> Edward Turley Smith, convict, Sydney, 1800

It's a pretty powerful statement to utter, when you've been transported for life from Ireland to Sydney, and are desperate to return home. For Edward Turley Smith, convicted highwayman and (coincidentally) Cassie's 5x great-grandfather, it was said in desperation to a fellow convict after he'd been in the colony for just on four years. Cassie and her mum Barbara discovered the quote in papers housed in the NSW State Archives. Edward Turley was on trial for some rather nefarious behaviour in the colony (that's a whole book in itself), and him uttering this remark to his convict colleague was one of the pieces of evidence contained in the prosecution. The statement opened up a huge revelation about his life in the colony, and there it was in the state archives, just waiting to be discovered.

In this chapter we'll introduce the state and federal archives and libraries and the wealth of information they hold, because that's where you'll be off to next in your genealogy journey. Getting familiar with all the main repositories and online subscription portals and what types of records they have will help you formulate a research plan and stay on track.

When you're researching your family origins, you'll be looking for primary and secondary records to document their lives. Primary sources are first-hand accounts of events and government records that documented and recorded details of these events. By and large, they are found in archives offices, though some are also in major public libraries. Secondary sources generally retell an event through someone else's eyes, and are usually recorded in books, magazines, journals and so on, using primary records as the source, and are more often to be found in libraries. These sources are great at giving you the context in which your ancestor lived and can offer clues as to what primary records you could look for. To excel in your research you'll want to corroborate and confirm anything you find in a secondary source with a primary source. Not that this means that all primary records are accurate either. A common error in primary sources is the misspelling or anglicising of names in official records.

First up, though, we need to talk about the history of the state and territory borders in Australia since colonisation, because this will affect where you go to look for records.

COMMON TERMS YOU'LL COME ACROSS

Agency The creator of the records, usually a government agency. For example, the Colonial Secretary's Office.

Index A list of what is in the record set, often done later, after the record was created. Indexes can help you find which original record is worth checking.

Item A single record or many records; for example, an item may be a single map, a family bible, or a bundle of correspondence (letters, telegrams and reports).*

Microfilm and microfiche Often collectively called 'microform', these two formats are scaled-down reproductions of documents. Microfilm is usually 35 mm or 16 mm film, while microfiche is a flat sheet film, usually measuring 105 x 148 mm. Both can be viewed on a microform reader; most libraries offer access to these facilities.

Primary source A firsthand or official account of an event. Government records such as birth certificates, military records and passenger lists are all primary sources.

Record Information of permanent and historic value, often in paper-based form (for example, a letter, photograph or map), but can also be a CD, a film or a digital file.*

Secondary source A retelling of an original event, often at a later date. Examples may include books, indexes and transcriptions.

Series A group of related items created, received or used in the same activity. Often a record will be cited as being part of a series of records that all relate to each other.*

* As defined by Queensland State Archives: qld.gov.au/recreation/arts/heritage/archives/collection

The evolution of the states and territories

When researching your family history you'll need to get to grips with the evolution of the states and territories across Australia since 1788. Many of the records you'll want to access are state-based, so which archives you need to look at will depend on when that state or territory was proclaimed, and which state or colony administered it before then.

In 1786, two years before Arthur Phillip and his band of not-so-merry convicts and crew arrived in Botany Bay, the British Government defined the boundaries of the first British colony in the Pacific Ocean without recognising the Indigenous population. They proclaimed almost the entire eastern half of the continent to be New South Wales, of which Phillip was appointed governor. The other half of the continent was referred to as New Holland.

From the settlement at Port Jackson on 26 January 1788 up until 1825, any government records pertaining to the colony are housed by the relevant authority in New South Wales. From 1825, new colonies began to separate from New South Wales and be proclaimed, so after the dates below, you should go to the appropriate authority in that state. That said, if you're on the trail of an ancestor close to when a new colony was established, check both. For example, if you're tracing an ancestor who was in Queensland around the time that colony was proclaimed, then it's worth looking at both Queensland records and New South Wales records.

1825: Van Diemen's Land became a separate colony from New South Wales. It was renamed Tasmania on 1 January 1856.

1829: The Swan River Colony was established. It was renamed Western Australia in 1832. Western Australia is the only state that has never been part of New South Wales, other than when King George's Sound (later Albany) was governed by New South Wales from 1826 to 1831.

1836: South Australia was established as a free settlement.

1851: The District of Port Phillip separated from New South Wales and became the new colony of Victoria.

1859: The colony of Queensland was established.

1863: The colony of South Australia acquired the Northern Territory from New South Wales.

1901: The Commonwealth of Australia was proclaimed.

1911: The Northern Territory was transferred to Commonwealth control.

1911: The Federal Capital Territory was established.*

1915: Jervis Bay in New South Wales was added to the Federal Capital Territory, when the capital decided it needed a port.

1927: Northern Territory was divided into North Australia and Central Australia.

1931: North Australia and Central Australia merged into the Northern Territory.

1938: The Federal Capital Territory was renamed the Australian Capital Territory (ACT).

1989: Jervis Bay Territory in Jervis Bay becomes a separate Commonwealth Territory, although it is administered by the ACT.

---

* Prior to 1911 the area now known as the 'Australian Capital Territory' was administratively part of New South Wales. Between 1 January 1911 and 29 July 1938 it was officially known as the 'Federal Capital Territory'. Generally speaking, for records prior to 1930, look at the appropriate records for New South Wales.

National, state and other public libraries

Many record collections that are relevant to family history in Australia are housed by either archives or libraries. The general difference between libraries and archives is that libraries are collectors of historic material, acquired because they believe it is of significant value to others. Diaries and private papers are examples of this. Government archives house records created by local, state and federal governments for safekeeping and documentation. Both have extensive collections that are necessary in family history research. Private organisations can also hold archives; for example, banks, companies and some families.

The National Library of Australia (NLA) has an enormous collection of material relating to Australia and the Australian people. As a legal deposit library, it holds a copy of every book published in Australia – legal deposit regulations specify that a copy of every book published in the country, whether by a publisher or self-published, must be lodged with the NLA.

The NLA is a reference library and its collection is held in closed book stacks, meaning that you can't borrow books to take home, and you can't browse the shelves – you must request items to be collected from the stacks and brought to the onsite reading room.

State libraries house collections related to their jurisdiction and are also legal deposit libraries for books published in that state. Some state libraries are also reference libraries, while some allow you to borrow material. Check with the relevant institution for details.

Often, local public libraries within a community will have resources and a local history collection relevant to that locale, including previously published family histories from the area.

ASK THE LIBRARIANS

We met with Melissa Jackson, a librarian who specialises in First Nations family history at SLNSW, as well as Peter Edwards, a librarian in the heritage and engagement team at the State Library of Western Australia (SLWA) for tips on using each library's resources.

Melissa Jackson is a Bundjalung woman with family links to the Baryulgil area near Grafton, New South Wales. She has a Masters in Indigenous Language Education from the University of Sydney and knows the collections at SLNSW well. 'Over the years, I've learned more and more about the types of records that we hold here and the types of records that would have information for First Nations people doing their family history.'

Melissa says that in most cases, you're still looking at generic historical records when searching for Aboriginal ancestors. 'Don't discount any record because you think "I want Aboriginal records". SLNSW holds published books about an area, for example, and usually the first chapter is about the Aborigines before white people turn up and so you'll get a really good history of what Aboriginal people were doing in the area before the colonisation. We have manuscripts, business records, diaries, journals. We have pictures, which can be invaluable, very poignant. And we have maps, which will show you where your family lived. We purchased a lot of church registers. So we have, for example, the Roman Catholic Diocese records, the Church of England diocese records, and they have those small little towns' parish records from when the priest did the circuit and they tried to scoop up everybody and Christianise them by baptising them.'

Another case in point are the birth, death and marriage records, says Melissa. 'It was law from the 1850s to register a birth, death or marriage. I go there. I go into the births, deaths and marriages. My canny tip is instead of a surname you put "Aboriginal" and then a given name and your area down the bottom. There are 350 individuals registered in that fashion. So don't discount *any* place that you could find [information].'

There's information hidden in plain sight when it comes to Indigenous family history, says Melissa. 'In business records, for example, on sheep stations: Aboriginal men were the majority of the shearers, Aboriginal women did the cooking. Aboriginal men did the boundary riding. [In the records] it's going to say "Joey Bloggs boundary rider". It's not going to say "Joey Bloggs *Aboriginal* boundary rider". It's hidden within the records.'

The same goes for military service records. 'Of course, Aboriginal men couldn't serve in World War One', says Melissa. 'But the stocks were getting low for our servicemen, so they allowed Aboriginal men who were probably my colour, and what they would say was in their description, it would be "dark complexion, dark hair, dark eyes", and that's sort of a code for an Aboriginal person. Sometimes it says Aboriginal but quite often it's just the description of the person.'

As with any family history research, advises Melissa, don't fall down the rabbit hole. 'Go from the known to the unknown. So yourself, your parents, and then your aunties, uncles. Don't say to yourself "Oh, I think my grandmother was Aboriginal and so I'm going to look into my grandmother" without seeing that connection between your parents and grandparents. Go from known to unknown until you get to that ancestor. Don't give up. Keep at it and look at it in different ways. You'll get there.'

Peter Edwards, from SLWA, has spent the past two decades helping researchers navigate the library's collections. And what a far-ranging collection it is, says Peter. 'We have a wealth of material and resources in the building to start people on their family history journey. Working with colleagues in the Aboriginal History Research Service, we can point people towards Aboriginal collection material, relevant state records or our Storylines digital archive. We have French and Dutch exploration materials. We have any number of colonial and settler materials, whether they be diaries, personal letters from settlers and convicts, ledgers, such as registers for marriages, births and deaths mainly from the various Protestant denominations. We have First World War letters and diaries and collections of postcards, and so many more various materials, such as tens of thousands of maps of West Australia that have been collected by the library, or collected and donated by private citizens, from early times through to where we are today.'

One of Peter's recent discoveries in the collection shows the power of looking at an original record, rather than a digital copy. 'A lot of items in our collection are keepsakes, such as family bibles. We have a bible from one settler, for example, that was published in the 1600s, and I went and had a look at it recently, thinking that there might be a family history on the inside of the bible's cover. And of course, there was; now, there is nothing like eyeballing archival materials in the hope of finding a bit more information. What did I find when viewing the bible? Well, tucked in against the genealogical list were three locks of hair from – as far as I currently know – three different people: kids most likely. And they still retain their colour!'

How to access passenger lists is one of the most frequently asked questions from the public; so too vital records such as births, deaths and marriages, says Peter. 'Hatching, matching and dispatching records are very popular – they're the ones that people will go for more often than not. That's really the pebble that starts the landslide, if people come in and they ask the question, they are essentially flicking the proverbial pebble, which starts the landslide of realisation about how much more family history research material exists.

'The important thing to remember with any of the family history material that we have – and there's an awful lot of material online, which is just fantastic – is that not everything is online, and that's why you need to be able to go into a library to access physical archives wherever possible. For example, we've digitised the Police Gazettes from 1876 to 1900. But we have them available up to 1972 in hard copy. You can get online and go to the post office directories on our catalogue, and they cover 1893 to 1949. We've digitised all those things, the idea being to make as much as easily accessible as possible online, and why? Well, the state is so large, not everyone can come into Perth to look at the physical materials. Unfortunately, not everything can be digitised in a short space of time. There is so much of it. That's why knowing which organisations to physically visit, or at least send an email to, comes into play.'

And that leads nicely to Peter's biggest piece of advice for those new to family history. 'If you can't find something on the library catalogue, always, always, always – did I say always? – ask our staff, whether you're physically in the library, or you pop an email through via our Ask a Librarian service. Ask the question. The only silly thing you could do is not ask.'

You'll want to get familiar with a site called Trove (trove.nla.gov.au), developed and run by the NLA. If a book exists in an Australian library, Trove will find it for you. It's also a search engine that can locate music, maps, photographs and recordings across museums and some other organisations. But the biggest reason that you, like us and countless others, will praise this wonderful resource is because of its freely available digitised, searchable newspapers – more than 1000 mastheads in multiple languages, and government gazettes that have been published in Australia since 1803. See chapter 9 for more.

Two other available features worth highlighting are eResources and the Australian Joint Copying Project (AJCP). The NLA and most state libraries offer free access to a portal called eResources, which opens up many, many online record sets, some from the comfort of your own home. Just some examples relating to Australian records are Sydney Benevolent Asylum Indexes, as well as records relating to adoption and obituaries, but it also contains free access to British and Irish newspapers, which can be a fantastic resource for tracing convicts' crimes and trials, and to look for shipping records of when passenger and convict ships departed bound for Australia.

TOP TIP Get familiar with Trove, a website run by the National Library of Australia. Trove can search Australian libraries, universities, museums, galleries and archives in Australia to find an item for you, be it a book, map, journal, image, music, oral history, historical newspaper or a record from the Australian Joint Copying Project. Trove even allows you to search archived websites.

Search for 'eResources' and either NLA or your state library for more.

The AJCP was an initiative led by the NLA and SLNSW to microfilm archive records from the UK and Ireland that relate to Australia and the Pacific. The result is that 10 419 reels of microfilmed records dating from 1560 to 1984 were produced and made available to researchers in Australia, records that people would otherwise have had to travel to the UK or Ireland to view. The project started in 1948 and was completed in 1997. Records copied include (but are not limited to) British colonial administrative records, such as governors' reports or dispatches; those from the Home Office, which was the department responsible for administration of convicts; and records from the War Office, which was responsible for the administration of British regiments serving in Australia and New Zealand for much of the colonial period. In decades past, the records were only available on microfiche, but now they are available via online searching aids. Visit nla.gov.au, then click on 'Using the library', then 'Research tools and resources'.

National, state and territory archive offices

Generally speaking, the majority of your research time will be spent looking at state and territory government agency records – those primary resources that recorded key events in our ancestors' lives. For example, vital records such as births, marriages and deaths (chapter 4), wills and probate records (chapter 5), and records relating to convicts (chapter 7) are all state- or territory-based. (It's important to note here that while state archive centres have records on births, marriages and deaths, the administration of these records are done by the

> **TOP TIP** One of the most common questions state archives offices receive is: 'Can I order a birth, marriage or death certificate here?' The answer is no – while archives and libraries will have records relating to births and baptisms, marriages, deaths and burials, the actual certificates need to be ordered via the Births, Deaths and Marriages (BDM) registry in each state.

registry of births, marriages and death in each state. So if you want to obtain official certificates, contact the registry in the relevant state. See chapter 4 for more details.)

Archives typically hold original documents relating to immigration, education and hospitals, wills, gaols, court documents – such as the trial of Cassie's ancestor Edward Turley Smith – and land records. These are usually in paper form, such as applications, maps, photographs, letters, journals, minutes, but can also be microform, CDs and digital files – and include anything relating to government jurisdiction and correspondence. Archive offices will also have government records relating to Aboriginal and Torres Strait Islanders, although some of these may be not open to the public without permission from the agency responsible for approval.

The National Archives of Australia (NAA) holds records since Federation in 1901 (although in some cases before Federation), such as official military and immigration records. It has research centres in every capital city where you can access documents, maps and audio-visual material from the collection. State archives hold records from when that state's administration started (see our list on pages 23–24 for dates). Some state archive offices have satellite offices outside of the capital cities. For example, Public Record Office Victoria (PROV) has a reading room in Ballarat as well as its main office in North Melbourne. The Museums of History New South Wales (MHNSW) has some records of key and local significance in their Regional Archives Centres at Armidale, Broken Hill, Newcastle, Wagga Wagga, Wingecarribee and Wollongong.

Before you visit

Before you actually visit the NLA, the NAA or a state library or state archive, get familiar with what records they hold. They'll usually have a 'family history' section on the home page. Read their online guides to family history and have a look through their online catalogues; many have searchable indexes to the most used record sets, such as births, marriages and deaths, shipping records, convict records and so on, that you can access from home. Many also encourage online queries about their collections through 'Ask a Librarian' or 'Ask an Archivist' portals, or provide email addresses and phone numbers for you to get in touch. (Just remember, staff are there to help you

> **TOP TIP** Give your visit to the state or territory archive and library the best chance of success by doing some prep before you leave the house. Look at their website for research guides and see if you can join online first. See what you can and can't take into the on-site reading rooms. It'll mean your trip is more focused and organised from the get-go.

navigate their collections, not to do your family history search for you.)

You don't need to be a member to access these online, though we would recommend that you become one as this will help when you eventually visit and want to access records.

See if you can become a member or get a reader's ticket online before you visit, as this will save time when you're there. For example, the NLA and the SLNSW allow you to join online and will post a membership card to you. A membership card will allow you to request books and other collection material to use in the library; print, scan and photocopy; and to use their eResources. Note that if you want to request access on site to special collections, such as original and rare material, then you'll probably need to bring some form of photo identification that shows your name, current address, photo and signature. These specifications may vary from library to library, archive to archive, so again, check the relevant website before you visit and make contact with them if you have any questions about accessing material.

MHNSW requires you to sign up for a reader's ticket to view original records in the State Archives Collection. You can apply for this online and pick it up when you visit. They also recommend pre-ordering any records that you want to view from their archives at least two days in advance. This gives them time to process your request and have the record ready to view when you get there. Other archive offices around the country have similar policies.

Check the library and archive opening hours and transport advice, and whether there are nearby eateries, because once there, you'll probably want to make a day of it. Most libraries and archives have reading rooms where you can work. Often they won't allow bags, food or drink into specific areas, especially where rare material is being viewed, but where this is the case they do usually offer secure lockers in which to place your belongings while you're there. Take a pencil and a clear plastic folder, notebook, phone or digital camera (restrictions vary, though).

Here's a rundown of each state and territory library and archive office. Visit their websites to see what is online and for helpful guides to using their collections.

Australian Capital Territory

The National Library of Australia holds the greatest collection of material relating to Australia and Australians and is located in Canberra: nla.gov.au.

ArchivesACT provides access to ACT Government records that are more than 20 years old: archives.act.gov.au.

The ACT Heritage Library has archival collections relating to Canberran life: library.act.gov.au/find/history.

Queensland

State Library of Queensland offers access to many indexes relevant to family historians, including employment, soldier and convict records, and a series of videos on researching First Nations family history, called *Who's Your Mob?*: slq.qld.gov.au.

Queensland State Archives covers government records from 1859: archivessearch.qld.gov.au.

New South Wales

The State Library of New South Wales holds many original records, from early colonial papers to First World War soldier diaries as well as the AJCP papers: guides.sl.nsw.gov.au.

NSW State Archives Collection sits within the umbrella agency, MHNSW. It holds records from the state government only, including the Colonial Secretary's papers – no private papers or Commonwealth Government records. Its earliest official record is the Charter of Justice signed by King George III in 1787: mhnsw.au/collections/state-archives-collection.

Northern Territory

Library and archives collections in the NT are grouped under one umbrella, called Library and Archives NT. Records include community collections, government archives, published materials and ephemera. You can also search the catalogue for records on, and in, some Indigenous languages: lant.nt.gov.au.

South Australia

State Library of South Australia has a range of collections and resources relating to South Australians as well as other Australian states, England, Wales and Ireland: slsa.sa.gov.au.

State Records of South Australia has collections dating back to the 1830s covering colonisation as well as First Nations family history: archives.sa.gov.au.

Tasmania

State Library of Tasmania has many collections dating from early European settlement: libraries.tas.gov.au.

The Tasmanian Archives is situated within the State Library of Tasmania and also has collections dating from early European settlement: libraries.tas.gov.au/tasmanian-archives.

Victoria

State Library Victoria has a range of online resources and guides to help you research your family history: guides.slv.vic.gov.au/victorianancestors.

Public Record Office Victoria has more than 100 kilometres of digital and physical records dating back to the 1830s and a lot of records helpful to family history are searchable online, including for those researching Indigenous ancestors: prov.vic.gov.au/explore-collection/where-start.

Western Australia

State Library of Western Australia has a wealth of records relating to the state, and regularly updates a handbook called *Dead Reckoning*, an online guide to family history in WA: slwa.wa.gov.au/dead_reckoning.

State Records Office of Western Australia is housed within the State Library and there are online guides to help before you start searching the online catalogue or visit the archives in person: archive.sro.wa.gov.au.

ASK THE ARCHIVISTS

We spoke with archivists from the State Archives Collection at MHNSW and PROV, two of the busiest archives in Australia, to hear more about their collections.

Emily Hanna is the Lead Archivist, Collection Discovery at MHNSW – the agency that looks after the NSW State Archives Collection. Emily says the interactions that people had with the state government records, going back to the start of colonisation, offer so much information to family historians. 'We get a lot of questions on a wide range of subjects. Immigration is a really big thing – there are always people looking for the arrival of an ancestor. Convicts. Land research is another one. It's changed a lot. With the advent of Trove and a lot of the online resources, it certainly changed the way that people research and they can access a lot of that easy-to-find material without having to come in. So by the time people do come in, they're looking for material that's a little bit harder to find.'

That's not to say you can't go into the NSW State Archives Collection if you're a beginner and not sure where to start. 'There's always an archivist on the desk (in the Reading Room) to help people get into the collection. We don't do research for people, but we do provide guidance as to the kinds of records that might contain information that they're seeking.'

Emily estimates about 4.5 million items in the State Archives Collection are listed in its catalogue, and around 500 000 of those are digitised, with more being published every day. The State Archives has partnerships with online database companies Ancestry, Findmypast and FamilySearch to make record sets available on those platforms, along with records hosted on their own website. 'You'll find a lot of our microfilm records available [on Ancestry]', says Emily. And there's more coming online all the time.

Records that are more than 20 years old are open to public access, unless a 'closed to public access' direction has been made. Some records relating to First Nations peoples, such as the records of the Aborigines Welfare Board, are closed to public access for 100 years. Emily recommends contacting Aboriginal Affairs NSW to discuss getting access to those records. If you're researching First Nations family history in the colonial records further back than the past century, then many surviving records are in the Colonial Secretary's papers collection.

Emily's top tip for searching the archives? Do some background research first, so that you know what you're actually looking for. 'Check in the catalogue to see what we might hold that can help you, and particularly for your first visit, I think it's really important to have something easy [to search for] just to see how the place works and how it all fits together.' Oh, and one more thing from Emily: 'Be prepared to leave all your preconceptions at the door because you never know what you're going to find. Keep an open mind'. And make sure you have signed up for a reader's ticket beforehand.

Jack Martin is the Manager, Collection Management at PROV. He says about half the visitors to the PROV Reading Room are people researching an ancestor. About 2 per cent of the records at PROV are online – that's about 2.5 kilometres of records. That small percentage may make you baulk, but remember, PROV and other archives around the country know what records family historians need to access easily, so they prioritise them. If you're searching for passenger lists, convict indents or land records, for instance, these are all highly likely to be already indexed and digitised. As Jack says, 'We know people want wills and probates, inquests and shipping lists. So we've done huge swathes of those in digitising partnerships. We'll also digitise things that have a broad value or need, such as the Ned Kelly collections or Eureka collections. And we'll also digitise items that are at risk. So we might say, "This record is fragile, and there's no practical way to make the original available without risk of damage, but we can digitise it as it is right now and publish it for ease of access". And then that image will always be safe. But there are also records that will never fall under those umbrellas – there will always be an audience somewhere for the minutes of an obscure committee or a detailed technical report on a niche area of governance, but we try to focus our efforts on records more likely to be used more frequently, or which have preservation needs.'

Jack's advice before researching the records at PROV is to think about how your ancestors may have interacted with the government. 'This is the key to getting started. Did they commit a crime and spend time in gaol? You may find their criminal trial brief or prison register in our collection. Did they die unexpectedly, or from other than natural causes? You may find their inquest in our collection. Did they go to a state government school? Or file for divorce? Or enter what was then known as an asylum? All call for interactions with government and result in records being created.' It's also worth signing up to PROV's newsletters and follow its social media channels, where you will see regular posts highlighting different aspects of PROV's collection, plus insider tips and tricks for your research.

Join a family history society

There's another thing that we would highly recommend you do early on in your family history research: join a family history society. There will be a small annual fee to join – for example, our local one in Sydney starts from $48 per year – but for the outlay you'll gain access to a network of experienced researchers, events and advice. Family history research can feel like a solitary endeavour when you're starting out, or becoming re-engaged after taking a break, and most societies offer regular meetings, open days and usually a fantastic library of local history books. The Society of Australian Genealogists (SAG) in Sydney, for example, has been helping family historians for more than 90 years, and a few of their experts feature throughout this book. SAG runs online and in-person courses for those beginning, or re-engaging with, their family history and has a first-rate library of resources and collections, many of which are unique to the society. It is worth a visit, whether in person in Sydney, or online from anywhere. View more at sag.org.au.

Just like archives and libraries, there are larger state-based societies, and smaller local ones. For the former, in Victoria there is the Genealogical Society of Victoria (GSV); in South Australia there's Genealogy SA; there's the Queensland Family History Society (QFHS); and in Western Australia, there's FamilyHistoryWA. For a list of family history societies around Australia, visit the Australasian Federation of Family History Organisations at affho.org and click on 'About', then 'Members'. Often, societies will have special interest groups that meet regularly, so once you're on your way, you may find it useful to join the 'convict' group, or the 'military' group, for example.

> **TOP TIP** Jen Baldwin from Findmypast recommends finding a community to step into. 'It may be a Facebook group that shares an interest in researching the same topic as you, or your local family history society that gets together once a month for coffee and conversation. Wherever it is that you feel comfortable is the place to be – and that community can really be a priceless gift.'

There are also historical societies across Australia, whose members are usually well-versed in the local history of the area. They too run regular meetings and can offer advice that may be relevant to your family in the area. For details, visit the Federation of Australian Historical Societies at history.org.au.

What about online subscription sites?

Good question. There are a number of online subscription sites housing millions of Australian archival records. The big four, and ones that you are probably already familiar with, are Ancestry, FamilySearch, Findmypast and MyHeritage. All offer the ability to log in and view indexes and records. There's also the Biographical Database of Australia (BDA), relatively less well-known at this stage but worth a look.

Ancestry is arguably the most recognisable online family history brand. They have record collections that span 80-plus countries of origin. They offer differently priced subscriptions depending on what records you want to access. For a good overview of what records Ancestry has, go to the home page, click on Search, then click on Card Catalogue – you don't have to sign up to do this. You can sign up for a free two-week trial to start exploring the records and then switch to a paid subscription after that, or most libraries and family history societies offer free access to Ancestry to members on site. We'd recommend doing the latter until you're more familiar with the site. Brad Argent, head of Ancestry Studios, agrees that accessing Ancestry via a library or family history society is a good way to get a sense of what records are available. 'It's a great environment to have a bit of a play without spending any money. And if you're doing this via a family history society, they have a whole bunch of people who've done family history in the same room at the same time. So you don't have to go on this journey alone.' Visit ancestry.com.au to start exploring.

FamilySearch is operated by The Church of Jesus Christ of Latter-day Saints and is free to access and search its records. All you need to do is register an account. It too has billions of records from around the world, including a comprehensive number of Australian records. Visit familysearch.org for details.

Findmypast is a British-based site with a large contingent of Australian records under its belt. It's a paid subscription site that offers a free trial for seven days. Jen Baldwin is a research specialist at Findmypast and is based in the US. She says the site has many records relevant to Australian researchers. 'The easiest way to access the Australian records on Findmypast is to utilise the All Record Sets page, which essentially acts as a card catalogue for the site. From the top navigation bar, choose the Search menu, then All Record Sets. From there, simply change the location filter to Australia and New Zealand. You'll find that most of our collections are organised by Australian state or territory, so it's easy to navigate to whatever location is of most interest to you.' Similar to Ancestry, it too offers free access at public libraries, and from home to library members – check with your local library to see if they offer this.

Findmypast has collections relating to electoral rolls, education records, passenger lists and births, marriages and deaths. Visit findmypast.com.au to see more.

MyHeritage currently has 297 collections containing over 100 million records relating to Australia. To see a list of the collections, go to Research on the vertical menu, then click Collection Catalog (US spelling), then on the left-hand side you can filter by location to 'Oceania', then 'Australia'. As with Ancestry we would recommend viewing this catalogue first to get a feel for which collections are there. It too has a 14-day free trial and also offers a Library Edition, so check with your local library if they offer free access to library members. Some libraries allow you to log in from home using your library card. Visit myheritage.com to start looking.

The BDA is a subscription site with a difference. It's a non-profit project that lists transcripts and indexes of original records and published biographies of deceased individuals who arrived, or were born in, Australia. It then links those records of life events to create a biographical report. From one report, subscribers can link to another biography on the site, such as to spouses, parents, children, witnesses, employers and employees, through the entire database. It's mainly focused on New South Wales records at the moment, but there are plans to expand to all states and territories in time. We'll cover more about the BDA when we discuss convict records in chapter 7, or visit bda-online.org.au to find out more.

So that's our slightly-longer-than-whistlestop tour of the major record repositories in Australia. It covers the ones you'll become familiar with as you march forward on your family history journey.

CHAPTER 3

Building a family tree

AT A GLANCE: *Family trees can take a little while to get your head around, but armed with some information and tips from our experts, you'll be building one in no time. They are also integral to help you pinpoint where to start your research. We'll cover the basics of building a family tree, and what sort of online resources are out there to help, including a visual example of a simple family tree to help people get started.*

> There is a reason why a family tree is one of our key tools in family history research. It's a really good tool for helping you document and structure your information. So in terms of the beginner starting the research, definitely build a family tree as the starting point. Because as you gather that information and you gather that evidence the tree gives you that structure to document it.
>
> Danielle Lautrec, author and genealogist

In our opening chapter we suggested you draw your family tree on a piece of paper, starting with yourself and going back to your parents, then your grandparents, listing any details of the generations that you already know. In this chapter we're going to start building a research plan based on those goals you already thought of in chapter 1 and setting up easy systems to organise your research. Then we'll look at ways to build and save your family tree in either a physical or digital form that works for you. These few steps will give you a really solid foundation for the research that you'll find over the next few chapters. And that means you'll feel more organised and can easily pick up where you left off if you take a break from family history at any point, without then having to retrace your steps and get frustrated.

COMMON TERMS YOU'LL COME ACROSS

Family tree A chart that shows your family and their relationship to each other.

GEDCOM A universal file format that means files are portable across different sites and software.

Legacy, Family Tree Maker and Reunion All types of software that help you build an offline family tree on your own computer and organise your research.

Research plan A sort of shopping list, where you work out what information you need and where you'll go to look for it.

Research log A document where you notate what records you've researched, when, where and for which ancestor so you can keep track of the records you've investigated.

Plan your research

Once you've collated your family tree with the information you have to date, whether that's with pen and paper or digitally, you'll have a clear idea about what you want to find out next by looking at the gaps in your tree, even if it's just you, your parents and your grandparents at this stage. Eventually most people want a pretty clear picture of each ancestor's life – from vital records such as birth, marriage and death dates, to where they lived, what their occupation was, when they arrived in Australia and so on. That becomes your research plan.

What do you want to know first? Is it that you don't know the birth or marriage dates for some of your grandparents? You'll want to start there before you go back another generation. And as you'll see in the next chapter, when we discuss birth, marriage and death certificates, you may get information about the previous generation from these certificates. For example, your grandparents' birth certificates may have the names of their parents on it – your great-grandparents – so if that's the case you'll have more names to add to your family tree.

Genealogist Danielle Lautrec, who we referenced in chapter 1, has been running courses on good family tree foundations at the Society of Australian Genealogists for many years, and has recently written a book on the topic called *The Good Genealogist: How to Improve the Quality of Your Family History*.

Danielle, who by her own admission is a born organiser, encourages her students to have a research plan in order to be more systematic and make the searches more effective.

'If you're planning research, list out your questions and your tasks and the repositories you're going to go to. So I start with, "What are your aims for family history in general?",

FAMILY TREE

YOU

Name: ....
Birth date: ....
Birth place: ....
Marriage date: ....
Place of marriage: ....

Mother: ....
Birth date: ....
Birth place: ....
Marriage date: ....
Place of marriage: ....
Death date: ....
Place of death: ....

Maternal grandmother: ....
Birth date: ....
Birth place: ....
Marriage date: ....
Place of marriage: ....
Death date: ....
Place of death: ....

Maternal grandfather: ....
Birth date: ....
Birth place: ....
Marriage date: ....
Place of marriage: ....
Death date: ....
Place of death: ....

Building a family tree

Father: ....
Birth date: ....
Birth place: ....
Marriage date: ....
Place of marriage:..................................
Death date: ....
Place of death:...

Paternal grandmother: ....
Birth date: ....
Birth place: ....
Marriage date: ....
Place of marriage:..................................
Death date: ....
Place of death:...

Paternal grandfather: ....
Birth date: ....
Birth place: ....
Marriage date: ....
Place of marriage:..................................
Death date: ....
Place of death:...

"What are your objectives?", "What do you want to find out?" Then you start crafting research questions, and then you put tasks that are more specific, such as "I'm going to look for this in this repository". The structure is your aims, objectives, research questions and tasks.'

It's really important to have a research plan so that you can reach your goals, while being as methodical as you can and saving yourself time when researching records or visiting archives.

Now, with all these wonderful things you're about to discover, you're going to need to keep them organised. And it'll be your grandparents who will help you do this.

The 'four grandparent' approach to organising your research

Now that you're all set up to go hunting for ancestors in the archives, you're about to find a whole lot of research that will seem to multiply rapidly. You'll need a filing system to keep it controlled and organised in a way that's easy to refer to and add new information.

The best tip we've heard for how to structure and organise your family history and divide it into manageable bites comes from Danielle.

'The technique that I think is very powerful and a lot of people adopt is the four grandparents structure', Danielle explains. 'So most of us have four grandparents. And that gives us a pre-existing structure in our family. So breaking your research down into those four lines is a really good way of organising and storing your documents.'

The other clever thing with this well-known system, says Danielle, is a commonly used colour-coding system, developed by American genealogist Mary Hill. Mary developed the following colour-coding:

- Grandfather's lineage on your father's side: BLUE
- Grandmother's lineage on your father's side: GREEN
- Grandfather's lineage on your mother's side: RED/PINK
- Grandmother's lineage on your mother's side: YELLOW

Some of the family history software that we'll look at in a moment even incorporates that colour system, says Danielle. 'And if you're a person who uses filing cabinets and paper documents, you can get manila folders in those four colours. You can get highlighters in those four colours. So it becomes a really good system. And if you're taking photocopies you just highlight it in the colour of the grandparent that it belongs to and you've got an instant organising system.'

If there are adoptions in the family or step-families, then you may have more than four grandparents. But the process still works. Just allocate a new colour to each of those lines to help you keep track of the different branches.

TOP TIP If you're like us, you'll probably be forever scribbling in notebooks about research leads, questions to ask, what records to go to next and so on. Get into the habit of writing the date at the top of the page, then taking a photograph from your phone of your notes and uploading that image to the relevant (colour-coded) folder on your computer. It'll save you looking through endless pages of notes to look for that one thing you're sure you wrote down somewhere.

TOP TIP If you're really clever and want to be super organised, every time you find something, or have a conversation with a family member, or visit a family history society to look for a record, log a research report. You'll be far cleverer than us, because we know we should do it but, well, we don't. In the report, note down the date, who you spoke to or which record you accessed, the family member it relates to and the physical address or URL where you found it. File it – or take a photograph of it and save it – to the relevant colour-coded folder on your computer.

Log your research forays, even if you didn't find anything

Then there is the concept of keeping a research log – where you note down where you've researched, when and why. Some genealogists recommend this; others don't. Danielle, for instance, doesn't; rather, she suggests inputting the research straight away into your software, along with where you found it and when. For more information, see the six-question citation rule on page 60. Everyone is different. Call us old-fashioned (and forgetful) but we kind of like the idea of having a research log where you jot down where you've been, who you were looking for and if you found anything. The advantage of this is, of course, if you didn't find anything to input you still have a record of where you searched. Everyone is different, so find a way of notating your research plan that works for you.

Building a family tree

It may sound nonsensical to start building your family tree before you start finding out all sorts of things about your ancestors, but trust us, there is method to the madness. A family tree, no matter how basic – it's you, your parents and your grandparents at the moment – gives your research a structure. As we've already mentioned, it'll be easier to organise your research, and will highlight where the gaps are so you know what to focus on. See our example on pages 48–49.

Danielle agrees that a family tree is an essential tool for documenting and structuring the information you're going to find. 'For a beginner to family history, building a family tree is the starting point. Because as you gather that information and evidence, the tree gives you that structure to document it. And it doesn't necessarily have to be an online family tree. You don't have to use Ancestry's [version] or one of the other subscription sites. You can do family trees on your own computer. There is family history software, [or] you could do it in pen and paper, but the tool is the tree, and that's a really good place to start.'

As Danielle just highlighted, there are a number of ways to produce a family tree, and it's up to you which you prefer. It really depends on what your aim is and what you're most comfortable with. Is this a creative project where you want to map out a few generations as a gift to someone, or something that you'd like to frame one day? Or do you already know that this will be a lifelong passion and you want to keep building your tree and adding information? Whichever way, there are online and offline options you can choose.

Let's take the pedigree chart you drew in chapter 1 – the line chart using pen and paper. That may fit your needs perfectly for now. And as you go back further in your tree, you can keep updating it by hand and keep it filed with your other documents. If you're going down the creative route and want to eventually print it out and frame it, then there are various templates around. Canva (canva.com) offers a variety of templates that are easy to follow. Otherwise, a quick search on your favourite web browser will produce other options.

Building a tree on the big four subscription sites

If this is more than a creative project, and you're after a family tree that you can continue to grow and prune, then there are software programs you can use, and there are the online family trees that the big four subscription sites offer. We'll get to the software programs in a moment, but first, let's look at the family trees you can build on Ancestry, FamilySearch, Findmypast and MyHeritage. All are good options. In fact, Brad Argent, head of Ancestry Studios, would recommend starting your family tree even before you search the billions of records on the site, for the simple reason that we've outlined previously – it'll help you organise your research and see where the gaps are.

'Building a family tree is great – putting everything in the family tree and then annotating it online and making sure that you've recorded stuff. There's been countless times where I've found a record and thought "that's not what I'm looking for". And then two weeks later, I've gone back to have another look at that record, and I can't find it. You know it's there and I just haven't got the search right. Thankfully, Ancestry has a "Shoebox" – a place you can store those records for future reference. So, I think absolutely using the family tree on Ancestry is a great way of recording information.

'You need to build up that tree and what you'll start to find is you get hints – you get a little green leaf that appears next to a name and a family tree [on Ancestry]. And what's happened in the background is algorithms are running away and looking at all the data you've given it and [running it] against the databases on Ancestry to see if it can find any matches. So it kind of does some searching for you, which is great. And it will pull records up. Now what you need to do is go in and look at that record that will be sitting behind a paywall so this is a point where you can take out a subscription and you'll get to see the record. And then you need to look at the information in the record and see if it matches what you know. And if it does, that's great and it can often give you clarification of a particular point.'

And of course, another one of those databases that Ancestry is searching is other people's family trees on the site, says Brad. 'People's family trees are wonderful because here's somebody who's spent decades researching their family and put their family tree up. I have done that. But there are errors in my tree. And there are errors that I found only two or three days ago; you've got to remember I've been doing this for 30 years. And it's an error because I got an erroneous piece of information. It's an error because I made a mistake and assumed this record was my ancestor but it wasn't. So the best way to think of somebody else's research is that it's like a map. Even though you know the direction, you still have to go on a journey.'

The other three sites are set up similarly to Ancestry. At MyHeritage, you can start a family tree by setting up a free account on the site. Input the family details you already know and MyHeritage will start offering hints and prompts from their databases.

Findmypast also lets you start a tree for free, and provides free access to birth and marriage hints as well. Jen Baldwin

TOP TIP It's a good idea to get familiar with a GEDCOM file – this is a text-only format that is compatible across platforms. So if you've started your family tree with one site and wish to switch to another, you can download the GEDCOM file from the previous site and upload it to the new site.

from Findmypast has this tip for those just starting their tree: put in what you do know, rather than having no information at all. 'If you aren't sure exactly where someone was born, but you know it was South Australia, then just enter South Australia. It's better than leaving it blank. The more data you input into the tree, especially in those first few generations before you get to publicly accessible records, the more accurate the hints Findmypast can provide to you will be.'

As we mentioned in chapter 2, FamilySearch is free to use and offers free access to all its records, so just by registering an account and starting a tree you'll gain access to billions of records. Whenever you're uploading data to third-party sites, always check the privacy policy and understand what is discoverable by other people. Most sites will let you choose whether to make your research public or private.

If you sign up on one website and decide you want to switch, all four will allow you to download your data as a GEDCOM file. This is a universal file format for family tree data that allows you to import and export your data between programs. As Danielle explains, 'While the GEDCOM file does not include images, all of the sites allow you to download images of records but you have to do them one at a time. So, I usually advise people to do this as they work; each time they find a record of use, download a copy to their computer and save it in the appropriate folder.' That way you can take your information with you if you decide to move to another subscription platform or to an independent software program.

Family tree software programs

The family trees on the big four sites are a great way to start and to get hints to possible relevant records, but they do have their limitations if you want to interrogate the data a little more. For instance, as you gather more research, you might want a report of all your ancestors who lived in a certain location, or the average age at death. Currently, the subscription sites aren't as good at pulling these reports as the independent software programs, which can do these types of reports for you, and thus offer further insights into your ancestors' lives.

Danielle Lautrec is a big believer in using these specific software programs to build your tree. 'I think it's a really good tool for both beginners and advanced researchers because it helps you keep all the information together, integrating it into one place, rather than scattered all over your computer. It helps you structure the information. It helps you learn how to create citations, and the family history software has a lot of analytical tools, and things built in. I know there are some people that don't use it, and that's their choice, but I think it's really good for beginners to at least try family history software. And it's like any software, you can use it at different levels. So a beginner can start [with] the fairly basic features of it. And then as they become more experienced, they can learn how to use the more advanced features.'

But as with any piece of software, you need to research if it's right for you.

The two most popular software programs in Australia for building family trees, says Danielle, are Legacy Family Tree (for PCs and newer Macs with Windows software installed) and Family Tree Maker (for Macs and PCs). There's also Reunion, developed for Mac users, which, Danielle says, some people prefer to Family Tree Maker.

Here's a quick rundown of what the three programs – Legacy Family Tree, Family Tree Maker and Reunion – offer:

- *Legacy Family Tree*: The standard edition is free to download and only available for PC/Windows computers, although it will run on newer Macs if you have software installed that allows you to run Windows on Macs, such as Bootcamp, Parallel or Fusion. Easy to use with simple navigation and a system for colour-coding files, Legacy also has an automated system that will flag possible errors, such as adding dates that don't match with information you've already inputted, for example, a marriage record if your ancestor was too young to get married at that time. Plus, it will search Findmypast, FamilySearch, MyHeritage and Find a Grave for you, and allow you to use hashtags in order to curate searches across all your files. Download the free standard edition from legacyfamilytree.com (just prepare yourself for a website design that looks like it's from the 1990s). You could give the free version a go, and if you like it, upgrade for more features, such as a relationship calculator and DNA markers to record your DNA findings. There's also a pretty comprehensive FAQ section on the website that should cover most queries.
- *Family Tree Maker*: This is available for both PC and Mac users, and is compatible with your smartphone or

tablet. It has a handy erase tool (called Turn Back Time) to undo information, and the simple navigation is good for beginners to get their head around. It offers hints linked to billions of record sets on FamilySearch and Ancestry, allows you to colour-code different family lines and upload multimedia files, and it'll even access historical weather data going back to the 1800s to tell you what the weather was like the day your ancestor was born. How's that for adding context! To purchase and read more, visit mackiev.com/ftm. There's no free demo that we could see, but there are videos on the site running you through the features.

- *Reunion*: For Mac/iOS only, this has a free demo mode that you can have a rummage around in first (with some restrictions), before investing in the full platform, which at the time of writing is $149 and distributed by gould.com.au. It's currently the most expensive of the three on the market. Features include the ability to add multimedia to your files and create custom slideshows. There's a handy feature that identifies relationships to you and others in your chart, and integrates with Google Maps to show where an ancestor was born, lived and died.

Each of the three has its pros and cons, depending on what you're looking to get from them, and what sort of interface design you prefer. All three offer the ability to download and upload GEDCOM files. We'd recommend searching for reviews on each of them to draw your own conclusion as to which one you want to try.

As for Danielle? 'I use Legacy Family Tree. I've been using that for quite some time. I have tried Family Tree Maker as well. I found most people use those two. It's really whichever one you're using you think is best because you're familiar with it.

I usually recommend that people try Legacy first if they don't have a Mac because there's a free version of Legacy and then if you like it, you upgrade. [Generally] family history software has so many inbuilt tools that help highlight where you might have inaccurate information, [and] it helps you add a lot of data and add your source citations quickly.'

Citing your sources

Most sites that we've just discussed will prompt you to cite your source for the information that you're putting into your family tree. But it's helpful to know how to cite something in the first place and what you need to include. Danielle Lautrec teaches the 'six-question model for source citations' in her book, *The Good Genealogist*, to check you have captured all the information you need to correctly cite a source:

1. Whose work is it?
2. What is it?
3. Who created it?
4. Where was it created?
5. When was it created?
6. Are there any additional details required to find it again?

Danielle's rule is to create your source citation before you start using the source. 'Because if you leave it too late, you'll never do it.' We can attest to that. So many times we've got so excited about finding a record and understanding what it's saying that we've forgotten to cite it before moving on to the next thing.

'And the great thing is, with a lot of the big databases now like Ancestry and FamilySearch and MyHeritage, they actually create a suggested source citation for you when you're looking at the entry', says Danielle. Danielle recommends adding the citation to your family tree at the same time.

And now, we hope you have a stack of manila folders, some highlighters, a library card for your local, state and national libraries, and lots of enthusiasm because things are about TO GET REAL. Yep, next up we're delving into the archives, starting with birth, marriage and death records.

CHAPTER 4

Birth, death and marriage records

AT A GLANCE: *Let's explore the records! First stop is births, deaths and marriages (BDMs). Referred to as vital records, these are the cornerstones of any family history research. We'll go into the why, how, where and what you can expect to see on an actual certificate.*

> Whether David thought he was the father, whether he just stepped in and decided to take on that role, we don't know. So that one search for that birth certificate opened up a whole new story for me that has been going on for many, many years.
>
> Genealogist Heather Garnsey telling the story of David Rivett aka David Reeves, born c. 1846

When we were discussing the structure of this book, we knew that we needed to feature birth, marriage and death records as the first port of call for family history research. Colloquially known as hatches, matches and despatches, these are *the* vital records that you need to look at to kick off your research. They will also enable you to move backwards to previous generations

COMMON TERMS YOU'LL COME ACROSS

Church record Before civil registration, the responsibility was on the local church minister to record baptisms, marriages and burials.

Civil registration When registration for a birth, marriage or death became the responsibility of the state (or colony) administration. The first to do so was Tasmania in 1838. Other states followed suit. See the list on page 68 for details.

because of the information the records usually hold. And as our expert in these records, Heather Garnsey, will illustrate in a moment, there are a few tips that you need to know to aid your search.

Finding a BDM certificate can solve a mystery – or create one! For Heather Garnsey, best known for her work as the Executive Officer of the Society of Australian Genealogists for 35 years and recognised with an award for meritorious service to family history in 2015, the discovery of David Reeves's death certificate created more questions than it answered.

Heather had been researching her own family, in particular a young girl called Sophie Baun, who lived in Dubbo and was born in 1882. Heather had cross-referenced those details with other research so she knew they were correct. With an uncommon surname like Baun and a correct date and place of birth, you might have expected the birth certificate search to be easy. It was anything but.

Heather takes up the story: 'When I first started doing family history, you just had to send what information you had to the registry and they searched for you. And several times we did that and paid the money and got back a no result. There was no registration for the birth of Sophie Baun. When the indexes were first publicly released, I spent a lot of time trawling those indexes. I could not find any birth registration of anyone who looked like she was going to be Sophie Baun.'

Then came the breakthrough. Sophie's family members found a photograph of a man called David Reeves amongst Sophie's possessions. Heather was told this man used to visit the family and Sophie's children had called him Grandad. It was the development Heather had been waiting for. 'I decided to start looking at David Reeves on the indexes to see what I could find about him. And lo and behold, I found a Sophia Mary Reeves with a registered birth at Dubbo in 1882. Mother Mary Jane. So I got the certificate, and of course, it's [Sophie Baun's] birth date of 1st September 1882.'

At last, the mystery of the missing birth certificate was solved – David had registered the birth of Sophie himself. On the birth certificate he declared that he had married Sophie's mother, Mary Jane, on 4 September 1877 at Dubbo. That was indeed the correct date of Mary Jane's marriage, but to someone else! So David Reeves wasn't 'Grandad' to Sophie's children after all. More on that in a moment.

Even allowing for the occasional incorrect record or anomaly amongst birth, death and marriage archives, these key records of life events remain the foundation documents for family historians. They are the bedrock of any search for an ancestor, as Heather puts it: 'Everyone has to be born and everyone has to die. So they really are those bookend records.'

So just what information is on a certificate?

Early records and those in the other states are likely to contain less detail, but are well worth the search. Just to whet your appetite for the search, here's a summary of what you might find on birth, marriage and death certificates in New South Wales, Victoria and Queensland from the middle of the 1800s:

- Births: You should expect to get the name of the child, when and where they were born, the names of the parents, and probably the occupation of the father. You might also find where each of those parents were born, where they were married, and how old they were when the marriage took place. The witness to the birth will be recorded (likely to be the mother's mother, or perhaps a family friend). You'll also get the name of the person who registered the birth, which is usually one of the parents. If there are previous children you'll usually get an indication of this.
- Marriages: You will find when and where the marriage took place, which might give you clues about their religion, along with the names, marital status and occupations of both parties. As a sign of those early times, women's occupations will often just be listed as 'home duties' or no occupation will be noted at all, but you are much more likely to find the husband's occupation. Another important piece of information is their ages, especially if one – or both – of them were under the legal age to marry. Then you would also get details of who gave permission for that marriage to take place. You'll get the names of the parents of both parties, including the mother's maiden name, and their father's occupation. And in many cases, you will discover if one or more of those

parents are deceased. You'll get the names of the witnesses, who will often be other family members, or close friends. Either way, you will have more names connected to the life of your ancestor to explore.

- Deaths: This life event is one of Heather Garnsey's favourites. 'I think death certificates are often the best one of all in terms of the amount of information that they're going to give you. [In] the early period [of the colony], you might get no more than simply when and where someone has died, what perhaps they died of and where they're buried, perhaps who the witness was and not a lot else. But some certificates, especially on the eastern seaboard death certificates, you'll get information not only about what they died of, but also sometimes how long they'd been suffering from a particular disease and who the attending medical person was. Plus, you will get the name of the parents, including the maiden name of the mother, if that's known, and you'll get the year and place of the marriage. The details then of their issue. So how many children they have had and most certificates will actually list out those children by name. You'll get when and where that person has been buried, and who the witnesses were to the burial. The name of the informant, where they lived and their relationship to the deceased. Crucially, you'll also get where the deceased was born and how long they'd been in the Australian colonies.'

Note that information around the person's parents on a certificate then gives you a start on the generation previous to that person. So you're collecting information not just on that one ancestor whose certificate you're perusing but on the generation before them.

What's the first port of call?

Not all searches for BDM certificates will be as complicated as Heather's, but it does illustrate some of the pitfalls. For now, your search should hopefully be pretty straightforward with the generations nearest to you on the family tree (unless your parent or grandparent was adopted – see further resources on page 245 for information on adoptions).

Look at the family tree you've started and work out what is missing. We're assuming you have the birth, marriage and death (if relevant) dates for your parents, but do you have them for your grandparents? Do you have a copy of their certificates? If not, then that's where you need to start, by going to the BDM registry for the state in which they lived. Hopefully your knowledge of them already, or through an interview with another family member, has given you enough details to locate them on the index using their name, the place they were born/ married/died and the date of the event.

As you work backwards even further you'll need some key facts to keep going back with each generation. Along with the surname of your ancestor, you will need to know where the life event – birth, death or marriage – took place and, ideally, an approximate date. The latter is important as there are two key repositories of BDM data sets that you will be searching from the early 19th century: civil registrations and church records.

Today, the civil registration of BDMs is the responsibility of the various state registries that were set up in the mid-1800s and, as you might expect, there are different start dates for each colony. We have created a list over the page of the dates that civil registration began in each state and territory.

Remember, too, that the various colonies and territories also came into being at different times, so you may need to search in a neighbouring state. See our list on pages 23–24 on when each colony was proclaimed. So check out both sets of dates to avoid searching an archive for something that might not exist.

Start dates for civil registration

Tasmania	1 December 1838
Western Australia	1 September 1841
South Australia	1 June 1842
Victoria	1 July 1853
New South Wales	1 March 1856
Queensland	1 March 1856 (for dates to 1859, search in NSW)
Northern Territory	24 August 1870
ACT	1 January 1930

It's also worth noting that until Victoria began collecting BDM details, the method in use in the other colonies was inherited from the English system. But in 1853, William Archer created a new procedure for the collection of BDM registrations in Victoria, which was later adopted by New South Wales and Queensland. The level of detail in these records increased considerably. It has been a boon for family historians. As Heather Garnsey puts it: 'One of the pieces of advice I always jokingly say to people is if you're going to have ancestors in Australia, try and have them from the eastern seaboard, from Queensland, New South Wales or Victoria, because their civil registration system is actually one of the best in the world.'

Civil registration records

The passport to your journey through a BDM search is an online index. If you find the entry for your ancestor in an index, it will give you the record number, from which you can order a copy of the actual certificate. The good news is that in the Registry of BDMs of every state except Tasmania, there is a comprehensive searchable online index of BDMs, and they are free to use. Although the Tasmanian BDM Registry doesn't have an online index, they have provided information to the Tasmanian Names Index, which is available online through the Libraries Tasmania website. There you can not only search the historical BDM indexes but you can also download the actual certificate for free. They're the only state that allows you to do that.

Another index anomaly relates to South Australia. They have a licence agreement with Genealogy SA so you do your searches on their website. If you want a copy of something you find, you have two choices: order it from the State Registry or buy a transcription of it from Genealogy SA. Both have fees for their respective services.

DID YOU KNOW? Each state has privacy restrictions in place for BDM records. Generally speaking, you can access birth records for up to 100 years ago, deaths for up to 30 years ago and marriages for up to 50 years ago. Predictably, each state has slightly different date ranges for each category, so check with the relevant registry before you begin searching their online index.

Other indexes

The commercial genealogy websites such as Ancestry, Findmypast and MyHeritage also offer online indexes to Australian BDM records and you can often access these for free at public libraries. But although they are useful, there is a caveat, as Heather Garnsey explains: 'I think it's important for us to say that [these commercial sites] don't have access directly to the registry, so they're not indexing the registry records. They are using those previously published indexes that were put out on things like CD-ROM [or microfiche]. So they have rekeyed those indexes and that can sometimes create problems, obviously, if there are mistakes made or records missed in the rekeying. It also means that the date ranges that they cover are not as up to date as the registries themselves. So I would always advise using the registry indexes for searches, particularly for more recent searches that you're doing. Having said that, sometimes you might just come across a really unusual name in your family history and you think, I wonder if that's just in Victoria, or am I going to find it in other states. A quick search on something like Ancestry's birth, death, marriage index will very quickly show that yes, there's a sprinkling in Tasmania in the 1860s. And yes, there are some in Western Australia in 1900. So they're good for that purpose. But I always think going back to the source, to the registry, is the way to do it.'

Early church records

Before the advent of civil registration, the recording of early colonial life events was the province of church ministers. The first instance of one of those registrations was on board the

First Fleet vessel *Lady Penrhyn*, on 20 April 1787, when a minister noted down William Tilley's birth.

So if you are searching in a date range before civil registrations were adopted in the mid-1800s, you will need to hunt through church and parish archives.

Bear in mind that each system collected different information. Civil registries recorded births, deaths and marriages. Church records collect details on baptisms, burials and marriages. So it's worth looking in both systems' archives, including dates *after* civil registrations began, as church ministers have continued to collect their own data to this day. Searching both the civil and church registers means you could get additional information surrounding some of your ancestor's life events: birth *and* baptism as well as death *and* burial. If you have found a church wedding in the parish records, the civil registration of that event will be the information the minister sent to the registrar.

Fortunately, in New South Wales, Victoria, Queensland and Tasmania, these church records can be located by searching the BDM indexes for each of those states, as we described above. Genealogy SA has a separate dataset for church registers on that site.

Church records will also be held in diocesan archives or individual churches. Many have been copied and will be found in family history societies, state libraries and the National Library of Australia, as well as online providers such as Ancestry. Please see chapter 6 for details on how to navigate church records. Although the chapter concentrates on searching for the sometimes elusive death and burial records, the search for baptism and marriage records follows a similar path.

I can't find my ancestor in the index

Patience and tenacity are good virtues for family historians to possess, as searching can be a very frustrating business. You know your ancestor lived in the town; in fact, he died there, and you have the newspaper cutting to prove it. So why can't you find his death certificate?

The answer could be as simple as human error, and we don't mean yours, we mean the person indexing the original record. Index entries can be misspelt, misfiled or plain missing altogether. And that's just the indexing – what about the original record itself?

Records rely on the accurate giving and recording of information, often at times of great stress, like the death of a close relative, for instance. But, as Heather points out, it's not just about the information: 'sometimes one of the most crucial pieces of information on a death certificate is *who's* giving the information. The great joke in family history is always be very careful if it's a son-in-law; you know, when someone's died, everyone's in a state of grief. And someone says to the son-in-law, who's trying to be helpful, can you go down and register the death? So he goes off to register the death, and you've got to ask yourself, would he have actually known the answer to all the questions? And you can often just imagine the discussions that took place, such as, where did your father-in-law come from? He came from Germany. How long has he been here? I reckon about 40 to 50 years. And that's what goes on the certificate: 50 years. So you spend the rest of your time trying to find his arrival 50 years ago, whereas he might have been here 60 years. You know, this helpful son-in-law is sometimes one of the biggest bugbears in family history, I think. But always we have to remember that we're dealing with human

> **TOP TIP** If you can't find something in the index, try as many spelling variants as you can. Say the name out loud and work out what someone might record it as; pretend you or the listener have a strong accent. You could look for: Mac and Mc; both parts of a double-barrelled surname; swap the first and surnames; maybe the name is listed as a nickname (Pip for Philip or Phillip); think laterally, it's detective work.

beings and they have bad days. When they were recording information, they could have given false information if it suited their purpose. We need the documents but we've always got to verify and check everything that we find.'

Certificate or index?

There'll come a time, probably early on in your research of BDMs, when you have to choose whether to just use an online index for the information, or to purchase a copy of the certificate.

We believe it's an emphatic *certificate!* The simple reason for that is: the increased level of information you will get from a certificate versus that from an index far outweighs the cost. That doesn't mean we recommend buying every certificate for every life event of every ancestor, though, because the cost of this will add up. Be selective; choose the ancestors who are the most significant. For instance, you've found the first link to a new branch of your family; maybe you need an ancestor's death certificate to cross-reference it against another document like a will; perhaps you have an ancestor like Heather's who has been telling untruths and you're doing some detailed detective work.

Certificates are key documents. As Heather points out: 'A lot of people think they can do family history just using indexes, and not going to the expense of getting certificates. And that really is setting yourself up for all sorts of problems. If you just think of the amount of information that you can get off one death certificate, the time and the money it will take you to try and gather that information from all the other sources in order to avoid buying a certificate, just economically isn't worth it. And I don't think you need to get every single certificate for every person. You certainly need to work out who the key people are. Ask yourself, "What am I going to get if I get this certificate? What's it going to tell me? Will it answer my question?" If it does, then I should try and get that certificate. Certainly.'

Where can I get a BDM certificate?

The short answer is the Registry of Births, Deaths and Marriages in each state or territory. We've compiled a list of their websites opposite, to start the process. There is a cost to purchase each certificate, although in New South Wales and South Australia there are cheaper transcription options available to you. The New South Wales Registry website lists the official transcription services which can transcribe the information from the original document for you at a lower cost. In South Australia, Genealogy SA has transcription copies you can purchase and, as we have mentioned previously, in Tasmania you can download the certificate for free.

TOP TIP Before you press 'add to cart' to buy any certificate, first check with the registry to find out what details you can expect from the life event you are about to request, as these can vary depending on the date range and state you are searching in.

State registry websites

ACT: accesscanberra.act.gov.au
NSW: familyhistory.bdm.nsw.gov.au
NT: nt.gov.au/law/bdm
QLD: familyhistory.bdm.qld.gov.au
SA: cbs.sa.gov.au/births-deaths-marriages
TAS: libraries.tas.gov.au
VIC: bdm.vic.gov.au
WA: bdm.justice.wa.gov.au

And what of the enigmatic David Reeves? Heather investigated further into his life and discovered other mysteries as well. 'One of them was that David Reeves said on Sophie's certificate that he was born at Windsor, New South Wales, and that he was 34, which gave him a date of birth around about 1846. I spent a lot of time trying to find the Reeves family in New South Wales to find his baptism but could never find it. Eventually, I switched to looking for his death, and I tracked him out to Nyngan. He died there at about the age of 96 in 1937, and the informant on the certificate when I got it was his stepbrother, whose surname was Rivett, and he said that David had been in the colony for 89 years, that he was born in England, and that he'd never married and he'd never had any children.'

David Reeves actually arrived in Australia with his father, stepmother and five siblings on a ship called the *Sultana* in 1856 as a 10-year-old. His name then was David Rivett. Why he changed it to David Reeves remains a mystery, as does the reason he left money in his will to Sophie and one of her daughters. But one thing that is certain is he is most definitely not Sophie's father. A DNA test has proved Sophie's father is a man by the name of Kelly – but that's a whole other story.

As Heather puts it: 'I think the moral of that really is that you have to check and verify every detail and you have to stop and think of the circumstances. When you don't find a registration that you're expecting to find, there's three things you've got to ask yourself. Am I looking in the right place? Am I looking under the right name, and am I looking in the right date range? And if you have one of those three things wrong, you often won't find the certificate you're looking for. We for years assumed that Sophie's birth had just never been registered. It had been registered. It was in the right place. It was on the right date. It was just under a different surname to the one that we were expecting to find.'

This story illustrates perfectly the joys and tribulations of searching archive records of any kind. It's highly likely that you will find the correct information you are looking for amongst the BDM records, but *always* question what you have

TOP TIP If you can't find a registration, there are three key things to remember. Is the date range correct? Is the place right? Am I searching for the right name? If any one of these is wrong, you won't find what you're looking for.

discovered. Remember golden rule #5 on page xvi: Cross-reference everything you find with as many sources as possible before you declare it to be true. And be curious when you discover new clues and names, as Heather was when the story of David Reeves cropped up.

We'll leave the last word on hatches, matches and despatches to Heather Garnsey. 'You really can't do a family history without knowing when someone is born and when someone has died. You need that information for a family tree. They are vital records in that very true sense. And they really are the foundation that helps you to then start to build the rest of the story and add the other documents to it. So, they're probably the most important record in family history.'

CHAPTER 5

Wills and probate

AT A GLANCE: *When an ancestor passes away, they leave a pretty good paper trail. We'll look at wills and probate records, what you might find, and where to go. Because wills are legal documents, and also go through a court system, there are several legal terms that we'll run through as well.*

> And then to pay the following legacies to Amelia Bertram of Kerang Widow the sum of Fifteen pounds to be used by her in such a way in which she shall deem most advantageous for her children.
>
> Will of Gottlieb Frederick Bertram, 7 May 1904

The majority of the records that you will come across in the many archives – like certificates of births, deaths and marriages; a census or a land record – will have been written by officials who are simply recording key moments in your ancestor's life, not making judgments or comments about whose life they are documenting. When it comes to a will, it becomes far more personal. While a will is also a formal legal document, mostly written by a lawyer, it's one of the few pieces of official paperwork where you can 'hear' your ancestor's voice – through

COMMON TERMS YOU'LL COME ACROSS

Testator, and the feminine version, Testatrix The person making the will.

Executor, and the feminine version, Executrix The person who will administer the will, and be in charge of ensuring the deceased's wishes are carried out. This person could be a lawyer but often it's a trusted family member or friend.

Testate A person who has died, leaving a will.

Intestate A person who has died, without leaving a will.

Codicil A small alteration to an existing will.

their last wishes as they are recorded. Who gets what share of the deceased's estate can be a signal from the grave about how they perceived each person – even more so if anyone was expressly left out! It's a snapshot in the life of your family – an insight into the relationships at play at that time.

The will of Gottlieb Bertram is courtesy of Vanessa Cassin at the Society of Australian Genealogists (SAG). Vanessa is the education manager at SAG and leads their Beginners' Practical Introduction to Family History course. Vanessa is widely recognised in the trustee industry as having extensive experience as a learning and development professional, so is a natural fit for discussing the ins and outs of wills and estate archival records. And as the example from Bertram's will illustrates, wills can lay down more than just who gets what from an estate. In this case, the beneficiary is given instructions on how to use the money and is such a rich source of information, says Vanessa.

'In general you will, at the bare minimum, find out when and where a person died and get a copy of their death certificate', says Vanessa. 'In the will, what you'll often find is names of relatives, which can be really important, especially if they mentioned things like married names of daughters. So you can often prove relationships by the way people are described or mentioned in the will. You might find out about children that you didn't know the person had, or wider relatives; perhaps they didn't have children.'

And information that isn't in a will can reveal a lot too, as Vanessa explains. 'You might get some indications about relationships in terms of who's not mentioned in the wills. Why have they only mentioned three of their four children – what's going on there?'

And then there are those extra details that can paint a picture of your ancestor's social status. 'The estate papers will give you really interesting things like a list of all the things that person owned when they died. And so that can really tell you something about their social status or the way the family was living. Some of them are quite detailed – down to the furniture in the house. Or what model car they had, and whether they left debts all over the place. You may also find out who administered their property after they died. Now it might be a solicitor or the Trust Company, which might not help you much, but if it's family members, again, that can help you with identifying the connections between your family.

'In one case in my family, I identified that the person who was the executor seemed to have the same surname as the solicitor, and it led me on a bit of investigating to realise that the executor was the local Lutheran pastor and the solicitor was his son. And so that led me on a little bit of an investigation into the Lutheran community in Bendigo [where my ancestor had been living], and how interconnected it was, and it seems from reading newspaper articles that this minister got a lot of his congregation to go and make their wills with his son who later turned out to be a little bit naughty and ran off with some of the money!

'Sometimes you get correspondence between the family members and the people administering the estate. If there's anything sort of contentious, you might actually find documents explaining what happened. And so sometimes explaining complicated relationships, you'll actually see letters saying, well, actually they weren't married. If they didn't actually make a will, then you'll often get certificates and family trees in there, which can be an amazing help with your research, because it had to be proven to the Supreme Court as to who the closest relatives were to then inherit the money or the assets. So you just don't know; wills and estate records are a little bit of a Pandora's box: you have those standard documents, but you can get all sorts of extra things. And a lot of details that you may not find easily in other places.'

But before we go any further, here's a quick Latin vocabulary lesson. Because wills are legal documents, and also go through a court system, there are several legal terms that you'll come across in your research. We have listed the main ones you will find on page 79, for easy reference.

Besides the final wishes of the departed, there is also a wealth of other useful family history information in a will. Along with the testator's personal details, you are likely to discover the particulars of their spouse, their occupation and an inventory of their estate. You will also find the name of the executor as well as the witnesses of the document.

But as good a source of information as a will is, it's only half of the story.

Although a will is a legal document, it's really just a formal wish list of what the deceased would like to happen with their estate. Before the beneficiaries of any will can receive anything, the will needs to be proven as valid. This is done by registering the will at the Probate Division of the Supreme Court. This division is sometimes also called the Equity Division. A court order, called a grant of probate, is issued, which confirms that the will is proven as valid and that the executor has the authority to carry out the directions of the testator.

The subsequent grant of probate packages not only contain a copy of the will, but also a detailed record of the estate assets to be dispersed by the executor and any correspondence. The latter might give you an insight into the family dynamic at that time, especially if the will is contested. All in all, they are a rich resource of hidden gems about your family, well worth the time and effort to hunt down.

Getting a grant of probate can take a long time, depending on the will's complexity or, as is often the case, whether its contents are contested. As Vanessa Cassin explains, probate can take years, even decades.

'One tip I would give people is that not everyone's estate makes it to the court as soon as they die. So I would also look years later because sometimes they don't realise the person owned anything. A common one is believing that the person owned their family home. So when they died, the next family member just moves into the family home; for example, it might be on a small farming property, and the next person just lives there and over time people assume that they own the house. And when they die 30 or 40 years later, if they had kids and they left a will, the kids will go to sort that out and they realise, oh, the house is in Grandpa's name. And so then you actually have to go back and administer the grandfather's estate first so that you can give the correct share of the house to whoever was supposed to get it from him. So if you really think there should have been an estate to administer, don't just look within a couple of years of when the person died. Certainly most of them will be there. But it's not unheard of to find probate papers 20, 30, 40 years later.'

What if my ancestor didn't leave a will?

If a person dies intestate – without making a will – it falls to the Supreme Court's Probate Office to issue what are called 'Letters of Administration'. These documents are the court's formal approval that someone can be appointed as administrator to divide up the deceased's estate. There are strict rules about who can inherit, and in what order, beginning with the spouse of the deceased. The rules are laid down in the different states' Succession Acts.

Perhaps your ancestor didn't leave a will because they died suddenly, or in suspicious circumstances? In either case, you would expect there to have been an inquest held in the Coroner's Court. If so, you will be able to find the coronial records in the state archives, confirming their identity as well as date, place and cause of death.

You will find indexes for Probates and Wills, and Letters of Administration as well as the Coroner's records in the archives of each state or territory (more tips on those searches are detailed on pages 85–91).

DID YOU KNOW? Until the introduction of the Married Women's Property Act in the late 1800s, a woman was not allowed to own property. If she got married and had rights to any property it was automatically transferred to her husband, along with any possessions and any money she might earn during the marriage. But that didn't prevent widows leaving a will - many did.

There's another category worth your attention too: Deceased Estates. As Benjamin Franklin once wrote: '… nothing is certain except death and taxes'. New South Wales was the first state to bring those two certainties together by introducing the *Stamp Duties Act 1880* – a death tax; other states quickly followed its lead. This was the first tax of this kind in Australia and has been referred to in a number of ways – death duty, estate duty, inheritance tax, bequest tax – but whatever the moniker, they all had the same purpose: a tax on the value of anyone's estate that became payable on their death. If your ancestor's estate had a death tax liability, you will find a record of what was paid in the relevant state Deceased Estate files. The legislation governing death duties was repealed in every state during the 1970s and '80s. The Commonwealth had also got in on the act, in 1914, with a federal tax called Estate Tax; in 1979 that was also abolished.

Unfortunately, as with most records, there is no central archive for wills and probate records in Australia; each state or territory has its own probate system. Which means, if your ancestor had assets in more than one state, the probate will have been registered in each of those states. So you will need to search the archives in each relevant state.

Because each state and territory has its own Supreme Court and their respective archives, we thought it would be useful to summarise the wills and probate details for each one. But just before we do, it's worth mentioning that you might find a will without any grant of probate. This could be because the estate did not have any assets or the value of the entire estate fell outside the limit for probate to be necessary. It might also be that the assets of the estate passed directly from one spouse to the other, a system called Transmission by Death. This category is also searchable in its own right.

All in all, you will have plenty to go at!

Where do I find wills and probate records?

In most of the states and territories, the probate documents have been transferred from the Supreme Court to the state archives and are searchable via their extensive indexes. These archives also have handy guides and webinars on how to use their collections. They are well worth a read as although there are similarities between each archive, there are also differences. You can also find these indexes in the state libraries and genealogy societies.

New South Wales (NSW)

New South Wales is one of the states where probate records have been transferred from the Supreme Court to the state's archives. Since December 2022, the Museums of History New South Wales (MHNSW) have become the custodians.

You will find probate records are also called estate papers or probate papers, but in New South Wales they are referred to as Probate Packets. These packets are likely to contain the last will and testament, and details about the grant of probate, including an inventory of assets of the estate.

You could just dive straight in, but if this is your first time using the MHNSW collection, we suggest you browse through their collection first. It will give you a broad idea of what it contains. As well as Probate and Wills, their archives also include Convicts, Colonial Secretary, Inquest, Immigration and Shipping, School and Land records. If you select the Probate and Wills icon, it will connect you with a range of options, such as guides, webinars and articles to show you how to search their collection. Along with information about their probate records, there are also tutorials on their Deceased Estate and Intestate records.

But if you are eager to get going, the MHNSW has a powerful search function also available under the Explore State Archives button on their home page. Type your ancestor's name into the search box along with the word 'death' (otherwise you'll be searching their entire collection). That might result in you finding some other interesting documents, which, if you are anything like the pair of us, will mean you get sidetracked from your original search!

Once you have found your ancestor in the index, look for the PDF icon on the left alongside their name. That will mean the original record has been digitised and can be viewed online. If that isn't the case, you have two options: view the original record in the Western Sydney Records Centre in Kingswood or, if you are unable to visit the MHNSW reading rooms, you can purchase your own copy from them.

If you intend to visit the MHNSW reading rooms, you will need to apply for a reader's ticket first. It's a simple process via their website. It's also a good idea to pre-book the item so it's available for you when you get there. You can do this by clicking on the black clipboard symbol on the above right of the record you have found. You will see another clipboard symbol, orange this time, on the right of the page. This allows you to view, edit and finalise your request.

For those of you purchasing your own copies of records, you can do this by selecting the shopping trolley icon from the line on the top right. You will be asked whether you want a hard copy or digital version. You can finalise the process by selecting the orange shopping cart on the right. There is a charge for this option.

Australian Capital Territory (ACT)

If you are looking for wills and probate records in the ACT before 1930, you should search in the State Archives of New South Wales held by the MHNSW, as the ACT was originally part of New South Wales. Archives ACT has a finding aid for Wills, Probate and Letters of Administration, which can be downloaded from their website. Since 1967, the Supreme Court's Probate Registry has kept a register of files – indexes are available for public access.

Tasmania (TAS)

You will find probate papers and letters of administration on the Libraries Tasmania website. From their home page, select Tasmanian Archives, which will take you through to a collection of icons. Click the Family History icon. Type your ancestor's name into the search box and see what you get. If it's a common surname you might need to filter your results by limiting the search. You can do this by selecting 'View All' under the 'Record Type' list on the left. Choose 'Wills' from the complete list and click Select. There's also a handy help guide on the page too.

For wills and probate records from 1995 onwards, your port of call is the Probate Registry at the Supreme Court. Use a search request form on their website. There is a fee for this service.

For records pre-dating 1824, your search should be in the New South Wales archives.

Queensland (QLD)

There are four registries in Queensland: Southern (Brisbane), Central (Rockhampton), Northern (Townsville) and the Cairns registry. Fortunately, the Queensland State Archives (QSA) holds many of the original Supreme Court records from each of the four registries.

The QSA has a searchable online catalogue called ArchiveSearch. They have an index of wills from 1857 to 1940 on their website. If you have a subscription with Ancestry and/or FindmyPast, they too have copies of the same index, albeit with some limitations.

There's also an online index of Trustee Files, with records from 1889 to 1929, on the QSA website. These Trusts were set up as required by the instructions in a will. You could find they contain records about school fees, conditions imposed on the bequest of land or houses, or details regarding a family business.

Another useful index you can search online on the QSA site is the Instruments of Renunciations 1915–1983. These are the records where an executor either cannot or no longer wishes to administer the estate.

If you are searching for more recent documents, they will still be held by the Supreme Court. You can search by accessing the Queensland eCourts Party Search system. There is a useful 'how to' guide on the Queensland Court's website. You can find it under 'Services' on their home page, then by selecting 'Search for a Court file' from the list on the left.

Victoria (VIC)

Those of you searching for ancestors in Victoria are in luck. The Public Record Office Victoria (PROV) is the home of wills and probate records for the state going back to 1841. There's even better news for family historians: not only have the records been indexed, the ones in the date range 1841 to 1925 have also been digitised – so you can view the original documents from the comfort of your own home. PROV is currently digitising the next batch of records, 1926 to 1950. You can request a copy to be made available at the PROV Reading Room in North Melbourne – this service is free of charge. You can also purchase your own copy, sent by email or post, for a fee.

One thing to remember is to make sure you view all the entries for your ancestor that you uncover. Up until 1994, wills and their respective probate (or letters of administration) were kept as separate documents. In fact, if you are searching prior to 1909, you might find your documents are filed in three places because the probate records could be in two different consignments. But the index should show multiple entries to alert you to this.

South Australia (SA)

The State Records of South Australia has indexes for the probate files and wills dating from 1844. But remember, there is a restriction on public access to probate records of 100 years. If you are searching within the last 100 years you have to go to CourtsSA. For the date range 1917–1979, access requests are via email to CourtsSA. They have an online service if you are searching from 1980 to the present, but you will need to register and get a login first.

The 1844–1916 Probate and Wills records as well as Letters of Administration can be found on the genealogy site FamilySearch. The records are indexed and you can view a digitised copy of the original online. You can also do this in person at the state records research centre at Gepps Cross in Adelaide, but you will need to book and pre-order before you go.

Up until 1979, a death duty, called Succession Duty, was payable on deceased estates in SA. The state records archive has indexes available online. As above, you can choose between visiting the research centre in Gepps Cross or, if you have found a record of an ancestor in the date range 1875 to 1935, you can view a digitised copy on the FamilySearch site.

Northern Territory (NT)

Probate records and their respective indexes are held by the Northern Territory Archives Service. You can search for a person by using the Archive Navigator. There is a guide on their site with information on how to use the system. Once you have found what you are looking for, you will need to contact the Library and Archives NT (LANT) to get access to the record to view in their reading rooms. Details are on their home page under 'Visit Us'. If you aren't able to do this in person, you can order your own digitised copy, for a fee.

You may find it easier to consult Ancestry's website, as they have the NT Probate Index 1911–1994.

If you are looking for probate papers less than 30 years old, you will need to apply to the NT Registry at the Supreme Court. You can do this by post or email, but there is a fee.

Also, do remember that if you are searching for someone who died before 1885, you will need to search the SA probate records as the NT was part of SA until then.

Western Australia (WA)

The indexes to probate papers, wills and letters of administration can be found on the State Records Office of Western Australia website. You will find a link to search the State Archives Collection on their home page. This will take you to the Archives' Welcome page, where you will find details on how to search the collection.

You can view the records on microfilm at the State Archives reading room in Perth, but you will need to register and pre-book access to your record. There is a guide on how to do this on their website.

*

Wills and probate records are sometimes overlooked as a resource to explore. We believe it's an area that should be in the 'must do' category. As we hope we have illustrated, they hold so much more than just the basic details. You will get a snapshot of what your family were like – where they lived, what they owned, and their relationships with each other. Another chapter in the story of you.

You will also uncover another stockpile of information to be collated and cross-referenced, so we would like to close this chapter with a reminder from our expert Vanessa Cassin from SAG.

'I am spending a lot of time at the moment going back and rearranging my electronic files and realising that I have changed the way I labelled them so many times over the years. And life would be much easier if I had actually just come up with an easy methodology at the start. I wouldn't have to spend hours now when I'd rather be researching. I think I just didn't realise how much I was going to generate when I started. Like I thought, oh, I'll get a few certificates, you know, maybe a few shipping records. And now I have thousands of documents. Sometimes I know I've got something and it takes ages to find it. So that is something I wish someone had sat me down and said, "Look, don't leap into this, actually map out how you want to store all this stuff".'

If you feel like this will be you as well, check out the grandparent filing method in chapter 3. You've been warned!

CHAPTER 6

Cemetery and church records

AT A GLANCE: *We've never met a family historian who didn't love a good cemetery. There can be a lot of information waiting to be discovered in cemetery and church records, so we'll break it down and show you how to use these records to overcome brick walls in your research.*

> *Duirt mé leat go raibh mé breoite.* (Irish)
> I told you I was ill.
>
> Spike Milligan, comedian and writer

You can find all manner of things on a tombstone. In Spike Milligan's case, it was an opportunity for one last joke – a legacy of his talent that will last an eternity. But the inscription, in common with many other gravestones, also lists the names of his four grandchildren, as well as his wife, Shelagh, and her dates of birth and death. Even if you have already found this kind of information elsewhere, finding it inscribed on a headstone is physical proof you have found the right ancestor.

You might not have a comedian or any famous people in your family line, but your ancestors' graves are still likely to be a valuable source of information about their lives and family connections. Inscriptions may describe how your ancestor met their end, give you an insight into their standing in the local community, or perhaps feature one of their favourite quotes. Whatever you find, it will give you a glimpse of the person beyond just their dates of birth, or death.

Uncovering the secrets in graveyards is something Petrina Prowse, from Capel, two hours south of Perth in Western Australia, knows all about. She's the President of the Capel District Cemetery Project, a largely volunteer group of about 10 locals who are working to document the 700 or so known graves in the Capel burial ground. While many of the graves had headstones, others didn't, and some were unmarked. So they did what many family historians dream of – they used a metal detector and sonar image mapping to go looking for graves.

Petrina explains why: 'Capel Cemetery is located on a sloping hill. It's basically on very dry sand so every time it rains, the sand pushes slowly downhill and covers up what might have been there, causing many graves to become hidden unless they have a substantial headstone or a grave surround. So with this in mind, in early 2022 the volunteers went out to the cemetery with a local person who had a metal detector, hoping we might find metal grave surrounds or grave markers that had been covered up by the sand.'

And even though this search only yielded a few small finds, they did discover something that would lead them to one of the older burials in the cemetery. 'We discovered a few red bricks that were poking up through the sand. The team worked and swept away some of the sand and this led to a discovery of two very defined graves side by side in the older part of the cemetery.'

Then in May 2022 they engaged a person to undertake a survey of the cemetery using ground imaging. 'That survey provided us with the location of 105 unmarked graves, some of which we already knew about, but there were many we did not.'

By now Petrina's team had compiled a list of all the souls known to be buried in Capel. While they had documented where some of them were buried, there were still many on the 'missing' list, including those two graves bordered by red bricks. One of the volunteers, Delma Cuthbert, knew that her distant relatives, Johanna and Frederick Roberts, were buried in Capel, but didn't know where. She had a hunch about the red bricks. She reached out to her relative, who was the 2x great-grandson of Johanna and Frederick. She was in luck; he was able to confirm that he visited their graves as a child and that they were side by side and had red brick surrounds. Just by engaging with a relative, they were able to solve the mystery of who was resting in the unmarked graves.

We can sometimes get bogged down in document and archive research, when the answer could lie within our own families. Along with interviewing the whole family, don't forget to look in those folders, archive boxes and cupboards that everyone has been keeping 'for posterity'. You might find letters and cards of condolence, funeral notices and perhaps even receipts from undertakers. It will save you hours, even days, of online searching or visits to public archives.

But I don't have a family archive

For the majority of researchers looking for their ancestor's burial ground, the starting point is likely to be their death certificate. As we point out in chapter 4, death certificates issued by most states and territories list where the deceased is buried – but not

TOP TIP Don't forget to engage with the cemetery office or local shire where your ancestor is buried. They will have extensive knowledge about the graveyard and its occupants.

all of them do. Tasmania is the exception, although that state does at least say where they passed away. We'll look at how to find a cemetery if you don't have a death certificate – or if you're searching in Tasmania – later in this chapter.

Armed with the name of the cemetery, you're ready to take the next step. If you're lucky enough to live nearby, or happy to make the trip if it's further afield, it's well worth taking the time to visit the graveyard in person, because a wealth of information can be discovered on the headstones.

When you visit the cemetery, you'll of course want to concentrate on your ancestor's grave or headstone, but take the time to look around you while you're there: where they are buried and who might be nearby could be just as useful to your research. Quite often family members were buried near each other. That could reveal another branch of your family tree that you weren't aware of. You might also come across an unmarked grave close by; it's not unusual to uncover graves of babies or young children that don't appear in official records. If one of these unmarked graves lies next to an ancestor of yours, there could be a connection between the two.

Quite apart from the grave of your ancestor giving you a sense of physical connection to them, the graves of other people nearby will allow you to gather information not only about your ancestor and their family but also about the area they lived in. You might find family groups with ornate headstones buried in an area exclusively reserved for members of that family: were they one of the dominant families living in the area? What did they do? What were their occupations? Was there a theme amongst the graves – perhaps many headstones referred to farmers, shopkeepers or business owners? This will give you an insight into the prosperity and social mix of the area. Perhaps some mention military service; was this an area where many joined up in either of the world wars? A visit to your ancestor's resting place will garner extra knowledge about the type of community your ancestor belonged to, which you wouldn't find on their death certificate or other documentation.

Remember, as family historians, we aren't just interested in the chronology or the sequence of events. As important as those items are, they just tell us when or where something occurred in our ancestors' lives. To learn who they were and what they were like, we need to understand the context of their lives. In this case, the event you are researching is their death, and where they are buried. If you take a wider view by exploring the cemetery as a whole you will uncover another part of their – and your – full story.

Creating the stories behind the facts is a huge focus for the Capel District Cemeteries Project. As Petrina Prowse explains, the group of 10 researchers wanted to capture the stories of those who were buried there for others to read and enjoy. 'Our team chose a theme called "the dash", which draws inspiration

TOP TIP If the inscription on a gravestone is hard to read, try an old trick: using a large piece of paper and a pencil, cover the inscription and shade over the indentations. You might discover what it says.

from the humble dash that separates a person's birth and death dates on a headstone. It seems small, but the dash encapsulates an entire life, experiences, and challenges. The aspiration was to fill in that dash so that stories of our ancestors are told for generations to come. We worked really hard using the records available to gather information and photos, and write stories that we then placed on our website. We hope that people come and make contact with us when they find a relative or a family member (on the website) and give us even more information.

'They're wonderful stories to tell. They weren't celebrities like today, they were just normal people like you and me and we just find it so interesting to ask why did they come here? And to discover all the little things they did to contribute to the life that we have now. They're really important. And when you find something about them, that's really personal and touching.'

CAPEL DISTRICT CEMETERIES PROJECT

Interested in the Capel District Cemeteries Project? Visit their website at capeldistrictcemeteriesproject.com.au to read more about Johanna and Frederick Roberts, and other lives the group has documented.

What if I don't have a death certificate?

Today, issuing death certificates is the responsibility of the various registry offices in the states and territories, but that wasn't always the case. In the early days of the colonies, it was a church minister or church official who was called on to

TOP TIP If you know your ancestor was Catholic but there isn't a church of that denomination in the area where they lived, your ancestor's burial might have been officiated by a minister of another church. This is particularly relevant in rural areas. If this is the case for you, try other local churches' records too.

record the life events of their parishioners – their birth, or quite often baptism; marriage; death and burial. Over time, these records have been transcribed by state civil authorities and are accessible, often online, as we described in chapter 4.

The problem is, human error has played its part during the transcription process. Some of the details were incorrectly transcribed, others had spelling mistakes, and occasionally, some individual records were omitted altogether. One, or all, of these instances could be the reason you've come up short on your search of the vital civil records.

The solution? Go back to the original church records. Which is much easier said than done, of course. Each state and territory has its own set of church records housed in a multitude of different places, because each religious denomination has its own set of archives!

You can give yourself a fighting chance of narrowing the search by finding your ancestor's religious denomination. As mentioned in chapter 4, your ancestor's BDM certificates may help with this. That way you can eliminate all of the other religions. Then you should focus your search even further by concentrating on the area or town where your ancestor lived towards the end of their life.

There are three main repositories for church records: the local church may be home to what you're looking for; they might be in the registers of the diocese; and others are held by the state libraries.

Fortunately, some records are online, along with the indexes to numerous others. FamilySearch and the commercial genealogy websites have links to many of the indexes. Once you've located your ancestor, you can get a copy of their burial notice – for a fee – by writing to the diocese. You can locate the various dioceses by doing a simple internet search. The Society of Australian Genealogists (SAG), State Library of New South Wales and the National Library of Australia have some microfilmed parish registers.

Something to bear in mind is the quality of the original church record keeping, especially in the early records. It was a bit hit and miss on occasions. For instance, places and names could be misspelt, so try as many spelling variants of either one as you can dream up. The accuracy of any record also relied on the diligence of the record keeper and their command of the English language, as well as how legible their handwriting was.

Another complication was the official's ability to understand different accents: for example, if they were of English extraction and were listening to a strong Irish brogue, it's easy to understand why names were misspelt. It could mean that the names on the family's shipping and immigration record don't match the details on one of their church records.

This was compounded by the fact that not everyone was literate in the early days either – if a name or place was misheard, bear in mind these notes were being taken at a time of grieving, there wasn't a way for relatives to check if the official had taken down the details correctly. It's not surprising then that when they were being transcribed from church records for the civil authorities, there were numerous errors.

All in all, church and burial record searching requires some rigorous effort. But don't let any of this put you off. If you do succeed, the rewards will far outweigh the time you have spent getting there!

I can't find a death record anywhere

If your ancestor's church and civil death and burial records are missing, or you just can't find them, there are other ways to locate the cemetery in which they are buried.

A look in the newspaper archive on Trove may prove the quickest option. Trove has a vast array of national and regional titles, all easily searchable online (see chapter 9 for details on how to use it). If you find your ancestor's obituary in a newspaper, it will usually detail where they were buried, and when.

Another online option is to search the databases of Find a Grave and BillionGraves. These sites include details and images of gravestones all over the world, and are uploaded by local family historians. Try typing in your ancestor's name and their date of death and you could hit paydirt immediately. Neither site can claim to have every grave on its database, but more and more are being listed every day, so it's well worth a go. BillionGraves also has a handy feature: it gives you the GPS location of your ancestor's actual grave, not just the cemetery it's in but its exact location. This is incredibly helpful if you're trying to find a grave in one of the larger cemeteries.

If you've exhausted all of the options we have suggested so far without success, there is another road to follow, and you

BURIED OR CREMATED?

If your ancestor search pre-dates 1903 in Australia, your ancestor will almost definitely have been buried. The move to allow cremation only came into effect in Australia in the 1900s, with SA being the first state to legalise it, in 1891. But the first crematorium in Adelaide, at West Terrace Cemetery, was only completed in 1903. Others followed suit over the next 30 years.

might have one of the biggest clues at your fingertips to help you. Do you know where they lived in the years close to their death? The majority of people will be buried within their local community, in one of the cemeteries nearby to where they lived, and most likely close to their relatives too.

If you don't have a death certificate or obituary, you might still be able to find your ancestor's cemetery. Begin by doing a cemetery search in the neighbourhood of your relative's last known address. Using your favourite web search engine, just type in 'cemetery' and their local town. Even if you live in a populous town or city, there's likely to be only a small number of cemeteries. If you have found a choice of cemeteries, you can narrow down the search even further by checking the date each cemetery was founded – not all of the local ones will have begun at the same time. If your ancestor's year of passing falls outside of a cemetery's date range, you can cross that one off the list.

*

Always remember, in the world of family history, you will rarely be the only one trying to locate something, be it a record or a grave. If you have joined one of the subscription sites such as Ancestry, Findmypast or FamilySearch, you may find that someone else has turned up information that's useful in your search. If you discover someone has found the information you are looking for, don't forget to cross-check – they might not be as diligent as you.

And one last important tip. Do make contact with the genealogical group local to where your ancestor lived. As the work of the Capel District Project shows, the more eyes searching records, archives and gravestones, the better the success rate. Your local society could be working on a similar project. So far, the Capel project has been able to fill in the 'dash' for 224 people out of the 700-odd buried in the cemetery. Groups such as Capel, and others around the country, with their thirst and nous for research, makes them a repository of detailed local knowledge for all to share. And don't forget to make it a two-way process; tell them what you've discovered too. Collaboration is the catchphrase in family history circles.

Chapters 4, 5 and 6 have focused on vital records relating to birth, death and marriage. Now we'll explore other records and periods of colonial history that may relate to your family tree.

CHAPTER 7

Convicts

AT A GLANCE: *Some family historians jokingly refer to convicts as 'Australia's royalty'. Convicts left a vast paper trail of records both here and in their country of origin, so there can be a lot of information to sift through. We'll include details of indents, government correspondence and musters, plus some little-known colonial records that can provide incredible details about our convict ancestors.*

> FOR THE INFORMATION OF THE PUBLIC GENERALLY.
>
> —The undersigned, with sorrow known but to few, severed from the wife of his youth, with whom he has lived nearly half a century, makes known that her mortal remains will be removed from her late residence, Sussex-street, to St. Thomas's Church, Enfield, Liverpool-road, on WEDNESDAY morning next, the 10th instant (January) at the hour of 8 o'clock precisely. And the Right Worshipful the Mayor, Aldermen, and Councillors forming the Civic Body, of which body he has the honour to be a member, with all and every other citizen, who knew his late wife, however humble they may be, will follow her remains to the boundaries of the city; but the

> honour will be considered greater if time can be spared to go the full distance.
>
> THOMAS HYNDES. Sussex-street.

Sydney Morning Herald, 9 January 1849

Thomas Hyndes submitted the above to be published in the Family Notices section of the *Sydney Morning Herald* in 1849. His grief at losing his wife after nearly 50 years of marriage is palpable. At the time he was a councillor for Sydney City Council, a well-respected and well-liked member of the community, and a wealthy man, having, before his political career, built up a successful timber yard in town.

He was also an ex-convict.

Thomas was transported from London in 1800 for committing highway robbery. He'd held up a coach travelling through Wimbledon Common, a spot frequented by highwaymen hoping to fleece travellers of their cash and belongings. Thomas was convicted and transported for life. But he had a skill that was in demand when he arrived in the colony – he was a carpenter and a joiner by trade.

His talent and good behaviour in the colony caught the notice of the authorities, who promoted him to oversee the timber gangs for the government. He married soon after he arrived and was eventually given a conditional pardon in 1808, after which he set up his own timber yard.

We were introduced to the story of Thomas Hyndes by historian Michael Flynn. The land which Hyndes was granted for good behaviour in 1831 is exactly where Michael's house is situated, 200-odd years later. Michael discovered Thomas's

COMMON TERMS YOU'LL COME ACROSS

Absolute pardon Gives a convict serving a life sentence all civil rights and allows them to return home if they wish.

Certificate of freedom This document was issued once a convict serving a 7-, 10- or 14-year sentence had completed their time. It was used to prove that he, or she, was a free person and had freedom of movement to travel anywhere, including returning home.

Conditional pardon Gives a convict serving a life sentence all civil rights and allows them to live as a free person in the colony but they are not allowed to return home.

Fond A group of documents from the same origin, for example, an agency, individual or organisation.

Indent Otherwise known as an indenture, a convict indent is the official list of convicts aboard a particular ship.

Muster The authorities gathered information about the colony's population by requiring them to assemble in different locations on specific days to be counted and to check if they were able to feed and clothe themselves or were using public stores. Convicts were also mustered on their arrival in the colony to have their descriptions and personal details recorded.

Ticket of leave These were permits issued to reward good behaviour of convicts who had served part of their sentence. They could work for themselves but had to adhere to strict conditions and remain in a specified area.

Ticket of leave passport These were issued to convicts who were on tickets of leave. It allowed them to travel from their specified area to another area in the colony.

story while researching the local history of the Sydney suburb in which he lives.

Michael is well known in history circles for his seminal book *The Second Fleet: Britain's Grim Convict Armada of 1790*. It's a tome of a work, detailing the biographies of the 1280 or so convicts who arrived on the six ships that comprised the Second Fleet – a particularly harrowing time in the transportation era, where a quarter of the male convicts died en route and 40 per cent were dead within six months of arrival. The high death rate was due to the debilitating conditions on board and the way the captains treated the convicts. Some of the convicts literally crawled from their transport ship onto the shoreline. Of these six ships, the *Neptune* was the worst. Most convicts were rarely allowed on deck for much of the voyage, but kept below deck in chains. Some were flogged to death for the smallest of misdemeanours. Thirty per cent of the convicts on the *Neptune* died during the voyage, and more than 50 per cent were ill when they arrived in Port Jackson. Cassie's ancestor – Thomas Gulledge from Somerset in the UK – was one of those on board. He managed to survive and forge a new life in the colony.

The best thing about having a convict ancestor? They left a fantastic paper trail documenting their lives, or rather, the authorities tasked with 'managing' them did. From the convict indents that arrived on board the ship with the transportees, to the early government records once they were here, including those that mentioned any reoffenders, there is a wealth of information waiting for you to delve into. In this chapter we'll hear from Michael Flynn as well as Carol Baxter, also an author and historian focusing on Australia's convict period. As Michael Flynn told us, 'It's easier to find details on convicts than on the working class, because the latter just don't make such an impact on the records. It's not until someone commits a crime that the authorities start keeping a lot of records on them.'

A brief history of convict transportation

Attend any family history event around Australia that focuses on convicts and the first question you'll be asked is not 'Where are your ancestors from?' but 'How many convicts do you have in your family tree?'

For the record, your Honour, Cassie has seven. Some of these were discovered thanks to Cassie's mother, Barbara Hall, who thoroughly researched every convict on board the first six ships to arrive directly from Ireland between 1791 and 1800. Across those six ships, more than 1000 Irish men and women were transported, and their crimes ranged from petty theft to treason against the British Government. As we mentioned in our authors' note, it was when Cassie became involved in editing and publishing Barbara's books in her twenties that she became fascinated with the stories and lives of these convicts.

Like Cassie, Carol and Michael also became interested in convict history at a young age. Carol began tracing her family history while she was supposed to be studying for the Higher School Certificate. 'I was intrigued by the thrill of the hunt', she says. It's the stories Carol discovered about convicts that have fuelled her passion for Australian history over the past few decades and led to her writing three books on the escapades she found. And Michael's interest was piqued at age 10 when his grandfather told him there was a convict in their family tree. Both Michael and Carol will be our guiding hand as we step through convict records in Australia.

More than 160 000 convicts were transported to Australia. This occurred between 1788, when the First Fleet sailed into Sydney Harbour on Gadigal country, and 1868, when the last convicts arrived in Western Australia, on Nyoongar country. There are multiple ways to consider convict transportation to Australia. For some, it was a brutal, heavy-handed regime that tore families apart. For others, it was the making of them – they prospered and flourished in the new colonies. And most crucially, it was the start of the colonisation of Australia, when the lives of Indigenous people and 60 000+ years of their culture were upended. There's a lot to unpack when it comes to our convict heritage.

Life was rough and ready for the convicts. Those who arrived on the First Fleet faced a landscape devoid of everything they had left behind. In the early years, the threat of starvation loomed large. And no matter when they arrived, they were tainted with the convict brush, often assigned to dubious landlords and harsh overseers, and bore the brunt of hard labour if you were a man, and relentless domestic service if you were a woman.

And were they really transported for stealing a loaf of bread or a handkerchief? Well, yes, they were. And silver buckles. And yards of calico. Some were just trying to survive and feed their families. Life was lived on the edge, and if someone had an opportunity to steal something, they would usually take it. Others were career criminals, well known to the authorities in Britain and Ireland for continually breaking the law. Some were transported for committing highway robbery (another of Cassie's ancestors), receiving stolen goods (yep, that's another one), or for sedition, treason and murder. Most convicts were sentenced to between seven and 14 years for smaller crimes, and to transportation for life for more serious crimes. The latter were never allowed to leave Australia, while those serving shorter sentences could return home once free. Most ended up staying here, though, after their sentence expired, some even bringing their families out to live here.

The majority of convicts were of English descent, a smaller proportion were from Ireland and an even smaller proportion from Scotland. But a few other nationalities were represented in those exiled, mainly from other regions of the British empire, such as Canada, India, the Bahamas and the Caribbean, says Carol Baxter. In fact, 'anywhere else where the British military had a presence. You could say that Australia's multiculturalism began with the convicts, including people of African descent on the First Fleet. So even the First Fleet had people from places other than England, Scotland, Ireland and Wales, largely because of the military, but not always. Sometimes you have French people who've moved to England, for example, and then convicted of a crime there and came out to Australia. So you have a huge amount of diversity right from the early days.'

How do I know if I have a convict ancestor?

It might sound like a daunting task to research – how on earth do I discover if I have a convict ancestor? – but working through the research principles we've already discussed, and knowing which records to go to, means that if you have a convict in your tree, you'll find them.

One of those principles, of course, is working backwards from what you know. But how do you know if one of your ancestors was a convict when you're researching their lives in reverse chronology?

The first is to look for tell-tale clues in the records you have already obtained. Here are four of the most likely indicators, put together by the National Library of Australia:

1. *The words 'with the permission of the Governor' on a marriage certificate.*
   Serving convicts could only marry with the permission of the Governor, so seeing this on a marriage certificate means that one (or both) was still serving out their sentence.
2. *The name of your ancestor in a convict muster.*
   Musters were routinely done to record the convict and civilian population for administration purposes.
3. *The name of a ship and year after the person's name, in a document.*
   While documents such as musters will also list free arrivals with their ship of arrival, you are usually able to distinguish a convict arrival because their arrival status will have terms such as convict, bond, ticket of leave, conditional pardon or free/absolute pardon. The name of the ship of arrival was recorded next to a convict's name, often as a way of distinguishing people of the same name.
4. *Noted as a convict in a census or other official document, such as Colonial Secretary's Correspondence.*
   The authorities kept many official records detailing convict lives, and wanted to differentiate them from free settlers.

There are two other clues that could alert you to go looking in the convict records for an ancestor, and they are ones that Carol Baxter recommends. First, take a good look at anyone on your tree who was born in the colony before 1840. It's highly likely they'll be descended from at least one convict. This is because, by and large, convicts made up the biggest section of the European population up to that decade. Free settlers did emigrate, but not in numbers to rival convict arrivals. As Carol puts it, 'For anyone born before 1840 in New South Wales, there's a strong possibility that one or both of their parents or grandparents was a convict'.

Second, a story that perhaps doesn't chime with the rest of your research (and is often passed down through the ensuing generations). For example, says Carol Baxter, if the family story says anything like 'my ancestor was a remittance man', then be suspicious. 'Or, my ancestor was the son of a baron and he married the gardener's daughter and he had to come out here. All of those stories are almost always cover-ups. And what's the cover-up? That there was a convict there. It was such a big deal. So people made up stories.'

It was common in the late 1800s and early 1900s to cover up any family links to a convict ancestor. This was mainly due to the fact that by about the late 1800s, says Carol, you couldn't get a government job if you had a convict ancestor. Which is pretty funny when you realise that in the very early years of the colony, many convicts were given government jobs because there was no one else to do them! Even up to the mid-20th century it was still regarded very much as a 'convict stain'. 'It had to be hidden', says Carol.

These days it's very different. Family historians are usually very proud of their convict ancestry – depending on what crime said convict committed, of course.

As Carol says: 'There are a lot of ways that you can actually bounce yourself back into the convict era'. So just like with immigration records for free settlers (see chapter 8), use a person's death or marriage certificate for details as to when they arrived in the colony, or a birth certificate for when they were born in the colony, and go from there.

Convict records in Australia

Convicts were sent to New South Wales between 1788 and 1840; to Tasmania (Van Diemen's Land) from 1804 to 1853; and to Western Australia from 1850 to 1868. Moreton Bay (now part of Queensland, but at the time administered by New South Wales) from 1824 to the 1840s, and Norfolk Island from 1825 to 1850, were secondary penal settlements, for those who reoffended after transportation. The last convict disembarked on Norfolk Island was in 1850, but there were convicts there until 1855, at which time any remaining convicts on the island were transferred to Tasmania.

Official records for New South Wales and Western Australia are kept by the state archives in the respective state. Records for Tasmania are kept by Libraries Tasmania.

But before you dive into the records and start typing in a name, you'll need a few details in order to understand whether the results that come back relate to your man or woman. You'll ideally need to know:

1 Which colony they were transported to (New South Wales, Tasmania or Western Australia). Dates of significant events in their colonial lives and where they spent the majority of their time will give you an indication of this.
2 An approximate date of their arrival, using information on their death certificate or obituary.
3 When they died.

That way, you can quickly discard any results that come up after their date of death.

There are a few key records in Australia once you're ready to start searching. We've listed these for each state.

> **TOP TIP** Knowing which colony your convict was sent to, their date of arrival and the date of death will make searching the convict record sets more focused. If you know their ship of arrival as well from other documents, then your search just got easier again.

New South Wales convict records

The Convict Indents 1788–1842 are a good place to start. These are the official lists of convicts aboard a particular ship. In the early years of transportation, indents only included the name of the convict, age (not usually stated prior to 1813, but there are exceptions), where and when they were tried, and the term of transportation. In the 1820s, authorities started recording additional information on the indents, such as religion, literacy level, marital status, children, trade and the offence for which they were tried, any former convictions, height, and physical description, including any scars or tattoos. These descriptions are a goldmine for family historians and really bring the person to life, such as this one of a convict transported on the *Royal Admiral* in 1835:

> Nose inclining a little on the right side, mole on right cheek, another on right jaw, scar right side of neck, four small moles left side of cheek.

The Convict Indents 1788–1842 are freely available to search and view on Ancestry as part of their digitised collection from NSW State Archives. They are also available on Findmypast – though you'll need to sign up for a free seven-day trial in order to see a copy of the original file – and the index is free to search on the Biographical Database of Australia (BDA), but you'll need to subscribe to view the report. Visit bda-online.org.au/sources/convict-records for an up-to-date list of convict records available.

Musters and censuses were conducted at various times in the colony from 1795, and are another great source to locate your convict. The purpose of these head counts was to keep a tally of – and keep track of – the convict inhabitants and to understand which of them were relying on government stores for food and clothing, and which were self-sufficient. Convicts were usually identified by their ship of arrival and information was also recorded on where they lived, where they worked and who they lived with. The muster and census returns that have survived are digitised and available in the Australian Joint Copying Project (AJCP) HO10 series 'Convicts, New South Wales and Tasmania, 1787–1859'. They are also searchable online at Ancestry from 1806 to 1849; and available to BDA subscribers; or free in State Library of NSW, ACT libraries and at the Society of Australian Genealogists Library in Sydney.

The records pertaining to the Colonial Secretary's Papers are your next port of call and full of information about convicts and life in the colony. As Michael Flynn explains, the Colonial Secretary was essentially the chief administrator assisting the Governor in the early colony. 'He was in charge of government correspondence administration in the early penal colony and right through for many, many decades. The

Colonial Secretary records have been indexed where people are mentioned, for example, a marriage that has taken place, or where a person is living, or who they have been assigned to. There's a huge amount of context in these records.'

That correspondence has been preserved meticulously and is indexed and searchable from 1788 to 1825 at the NSW State Archives (mhnsw.au/archive/subjects/colonial-secretary), and is one of the free record sets that is searchable on Ancestry. The 'Colonial Secretary Letters Received, 1826–1896' has also been partially indexed and is searchable at NSW State Archives (mhnsw.au/indexes/colonial-secretary/colonial-secretary-letters-received-1826-1896).

On arrival, convicts were assigned to a household of an individual in the colony, or retained by the government. Men were often assigned as labourers or tradesmen, while women usually became domestic servants and housekeepers. In the 1820s and 1830s, assignment is often recorded on the arrival muster (or indent) and the musters 1800–1837 are extensive records of assignment because they tell you who the serving convict was assigned to. For more details on convict assignment, visit the NSW State Archives section on 'Convict assignment records' at mhnsw.au/guides/convict-assignment-records.

Some convicts were allowed to work for themselves on arrival, if they could show they could support themselves. Cassie's fifth great-grandfather Edward Turley Smith, who arrived in 1796, was one of these. In 1797, Cassie's 5x great-grandmother Jane Maher (who arrived on the *Britannia* that same year) was immediately assigned to Turley Smith. This was discovered on a surviving document from the period called 'List of Women Assigned 1798'. This means we can place Jane's whereabouts shortly after her arrival, and gives us a paper trail in which we can document their relationship in the colony.

The importance of these records – indents, musters and censuses, and the Colonial Secretary's Papers – all help you to place your ancestor in a particular geographical space or locality that helps you identify them, says Michael. 'That's what these records hold together. Convicts, especially the First, Second and Third Fleets, are very well documented these days, but you still need to be able to trace your man or woman to know that you have the one pertaining to your family tree. I have always regarded it similar to the process of deduction used by Miss Marple and Hercule Poirot in the Agatha Christie novels that I read as a teenager of the rational analysis of evidence to see whether something is possible and is capable of being proved and is sufficiently supported by evidence that it occurred. Family history is that kind of deep analysis and sometimes it's easy, sometimes people have done a huge amount of research and it's very well documented. But you still need to do your own checks.'

These are the main records but there are many, many other record sets relating to convict records at NSW State Archives, and on Ancestry and Findmypast. These include indexes to tickets of leave, conditional and absolute pardons, certificates of leave, registers of convicts' applications to marry, and criminal and civil convictions in the colony (convicts were fond of suing the pants off each other, forging promissory notes and breaking the peace, so were often hauled in front of the local magistrate), just to name a few. Read the guides available at the NSW State Archives, the National Library of Australia and state libraries, and look at the Australian Convict Collection on Ancestry to see the full spectrum of records available. And remember, you can gain free access to Ancestry's library edition on site at most libraries and archives. Findmypast offers access via libraries and you often don't need to be onsite to access.

Tasmanian convict records

Between 1804 and 1853, about 76 000 convicts were transported to Tasmania, then referred to as Van Diemen's Land. Until 1818, the majority of convicts arriving on Tasmanian shores were those who had committed crimes in New South Wales. After that, convicts arrived directly from England. Many records pertaining to Tasmanian convicts are searchable online at Libraries Tasmania, including musters, assignment lists and indents. For details and a comprehensive list of the records available, visit libraries.tas.gov.au/family-history. There you'll find the Tasmanian Names Index, probably your best, first port of call as it searches across many record sets. You can also read more about convict records under a tab called 'Convict Heritage'.

Western Australian convict records

Transportation to Western Australia (the Swan River Colony) occurred between 1850 and 1868, after which transportation to Australia ceased altogether. State Records Office WA hold records relating to this era, from the first ship, the *Scindian*, with 75 male convicts on board, to the last, the *Hougoumont*, with 229 convicts on board. In between those years, just under 10 000 convicts were shipped to the colony. Again, there are many record sets relating to convicts, from transportation registers, ticket of leave registers, good conduct lists and medical records. For a full list, visit wa.gov.au/organisation/state-records-office-of-western-australia/convicts.

Australian Joint Copying Project (AJCP)

We've highlighted the AJCP a bit, because it is one of the most rewarding record sets. And it's freely available. As mentioned in chapter 2, this mammoth project conducted with the NLA, SLNSW and the British Government sought to copy and document all records pertaining to Australia and the Pacific. For convict research, the main ones you want to look at are in the UK Public Record Office (PRO) series – records from the Home Office, the Colonial Office and the Admiralty. Previously the AJCP was only available on microfilm. Now it's digitised and available on Trove. Let us say that again – it's digitised and available on Trove! It's important to note here that the digitised material isn't indexed, but is listed by the originating department. So for example if you want to look at the digitised records relating to convicts from the Home Office, you would go to the AJCP portal at the NLA website, click on AJCP PRO Series, click on Home Office, then look at the records available. There are also digitised handbooks within each section to describe the material and guide you. Visit nla.gov.au/australian-joint-copying-project for more information.

Biographical Database of Australia (BDA)

Another essential resource for piecing together the life of your convict is the BDA. Both Carol Baxter and Michael Flynn have contributed their knowledge and skills to the project for a number of years. Michael is currently the BDA's Assistant Editor and Honorary Research Officer.

The aim of the team behind the BDA is to link biographies of every deceased individual who arrived or was born in

Australia to original sources and archive documents. As Michael explains, 'The BDA site is based on transcribing little snippets from a bit of an archival record mentioning a person and linking them together to profile a timeline for that person. The snippets can be a published record, like a newspaper item, or it can be an official government record. Eventually they'll all be linked.'

There are more than 2.2 million searchable names in the database already and work is ongoing to expand this number. 'The BDA has full transcripts of most muster and indent records, and even with a free search you can see clues such as year and county of birth', says Michael. 'The BDA also cross-indexes all the weird and wonderful ways names are spelt in the record for the same person. We also have index references to many trial records of colonial courts, which are key evidence for convicts who reoffend or were victims or witnesses in the colony.'

The current focus is on compiling biographies for about 191 000 people, mainly colonists and First Nations people who had contact with colonists, who were living in New South Wales by 1841. That milestone is within reach, says Michael.

If you're tracing an ancestor in the early colony, you may find that the BDA has done some of your research for you. Or it could be the first resource you try – as long as you know that when you type in a name and the BDA retrieves multiple results, you know which name on the results is *your* ancestor as opposed to someone else, especially if he or she has a common name.

An example of the work being done on the BDA website is for Maria Lock. Another site, the Australian Dictionary of Biography (ADB) explains that Maria:

> ... was born at Richmond Bottoms, on the eastern floodplain of the Hawkesbury River, daughter of Yarramundi, 'Chief of the Richmond Tribes'. The family belonged to the Boorooberongal clan of the D(h)arug people. On 28 December 1814 Yarramundi's clan attended the inaugural annual conference hosted for the Aborigines by Governor Lachlan Macquarie. On the same date Maria was admitted to the Native Institution, for tuition by William and Elizabeth Shelley.

As Michael explains, 'Maria was one of the early students, and in fact, was a star student at the Parramatta Native Institution, a school for Aboriginal children. She married legally a convict called Robert Lock and had a large family. Maria was granted and became a property holder of land, and appears in many records relating to these events.'

From Maria's biography we can see that Robert Lock was an illiterate convict and a carpenter who had been assigned to work on the construction of the new Native Institution buildings at Black Town (Blacktown) in 1823. The marriage was the first officially sanctioned union between a convict and an Aboriginal woman, and Robert was assigned to her. The couple had 10 children throughout their relationship, nine of whom survived to adulthood. Maria requested and was granted many acres of land around Liverpool and Blacktown on behalf of Robert. The land was divided between her children on her death in 1878. As the ADB explains, these areas '... were occupied by her descendants until about 1920, by which time the freehold land was considered to be an Aboriginal reserve (Plumpton), and was revoked by the Aborigines Protection Board. Dozens of families in 2005 trace their descent through

Maria to Yarramundi and to his father Gomebeeree, an unbroken link stretching back to the 1740s.'

Biographies such as Maria's on the BDA site show how people's lives in the early colony intertwined, which gives family historians huge context. As Michael explains, 'Maria can be traced as an Aboriginal person in records that have been linked on BDA to form a Biographical Report, beginning with a transcript of her marriage to Robert Lock at Parramatta in 1824. She then appears as the mother of her child baptised by the Rev Robert Cartwright at Liverpool in 1826, then as an employee of Cartwright at the Liverpool Orphan School in the 1828 census, and again as the mother of a child baptised in 1829. After these primary sources, two secondary sources are listed: firstly, a form summarising details of Maria's life contributed to the Australian Biographical and Genealogical Record by a descendant in the 1980s (now held by the Society of Australian Genealogists), which notes her death near Blacktown, New South Wales, in 1878, and secondly, a summary of Maria's entry in the ADB with a link to the ADB website, which includes a digitised version of her biography. Her Aboriginal ethnicity is noted and indexed by BDA, which includes ethnicity as an advanced search term, along with year, place, year of birth, death, arrival in Australia, arrival status (for example, convict, free, military) religion, employment and more. These can all assist in filtering information to distinguish individuals of the same name.'

And this ability to understand who's who is a key strength of the BDA: 'The biographical database that is being compiled and expanded is helping people to search for ancestors in that crowd and to distinguish them from one another', says Michael. 'Because in family history, that is one of the primary challenges.'

Carol Baxter agrees. 'These days when I'm researching a colonial person, I make it easy on myself. I go straight to the BDA to see what's there.'

The BDA is a non-profit subscription site. Searching the entries on the database is free, but in order to see the reports on each entry, you'll need to pay a small annual fee to subscribe.

Before transportation – trials and convictions

As you'd expect, there has also been an explosion of digitised records relating to convicts prior to transportation. While the scope of this guide is an introduction to Australian records, it would be remiss of us to not mention records pertaining to a convict before transportation. Because half the fun of researching a convict is finding out about the crime, trial and any previous convictions in the 'Old Country'. There are two main repositories that we'd recommend searching for these details – court and prison records, and contemporary newspapers.

Court and prison records

If your convict originated from England, then try The Proceedings of the Old Bailey, an online searchable database of criminal trials held at the Old Bailey from 1674 to 1913. Visit oldbaileyonline.org to start searching. Michael Flynn says the related Londonlives site is also essential for London research. Visit londonlives.org, then click on 'Search', then 'Person Name Search'.

Ancestry has records relating to trials including England & Wales Criminal Registers 1792–1892; UK Criminal Records, 1780–1871; UK Prison Commission Records, 1770–1951; and UK Calendar of Prisoners, 1868–1929. To access the collections, go to Search Card Catalogue, then 'Court, Land, Wills & Financial', then filter by location to the United Kingdom. So too Findmypast has a number of relevant data sets, including England & Wales, Crime, Prisons & Punishment, 1770–1935; Irish Prison Registers 1790–1924; and Yorkshire, Sheffield Crime Courts and Convicts 1737–1938.

The AJCP has records pertaining to criminal trials in series HO 7, 8, 9, 10, 11, 13, 16, 25, 26 and 27. For more information and links, we'd recommend reading The National Library of Australia's online guide to trial records at nla.gov.au/research-guides/convicts/trial-records.

For Irish convicts, not many government records have survived prior to 1836 due to the fire caused by fighting in the 1922 Civil War that destroyed most archives of the legal system housed there at the time. What survived is held by the National Archives of Ireland, including:

- Transportation Registers, 1836–1857 (M 2125–M 2129)
- Prisoners' Petitions and Cases, 1788–1836 (M 2130–M 2143)
- State Prisoners' Petitions, 1798–1799 (M 2144–2149)
- Convict Reference Files, 1836–1856: 1865–1868 (M 2150–2225)
- Male Convict Register, 1842–1847 (M 2228)
- Register of Convicts on Convict Ships, 1851–1853 (M 2228).

TOP TIP When searching for trial or conviction information, search more than just the year prior to transportation. Often convicts languished for two to three years or longer in prison before being transported. Barbara Hall found some Irish convicts were incarcerated for up to five years before being sent to New South Wales. Carol Baxter says that one of her ancestors arrived six years after being given a seven-year sentence and one of her husband's ancestors was never transported.

These record sets are also available to read at the AJCP on Trove – the M number in brackets after the record refers to the series in the AJCP.

The Prisoners' Petitions and Cases is worth searching if you're looking at a convict before 1836. These records relate to petitions from the convict or their family for leniency and can be fruitful in the absence of the transportation registers.

Michael Flynn says the Chief Secretary's Office Registered Papers (CSORP) at the National Archives of Ireland is also worth checking out. CSORP consists mainly of incoming correspondence of the Chief Secretary's Office in the early 19th century. This correspondence includes letters, petitions, memorials, memoranda, affidavits, recommendations, accounts, reports and returns, and was usually addressed to one of three officials – the Lord Lieutenant, Chief Secretary or Under Secretary. Visit csorp.nationalarchives.ie to discover more and search the catalogue.

Newspaper accounts of trials and convictions

Newspapers reported zealously on the crimes and trials at the various courts and assizes. They are a fantastic resource and can add much colour to the information, but it's important to remember that trials, particularly high-profile cases such as treason, were often hyped up and used as a form of entertainment for the reader. That said, newspapers are well worth searching for information on your ancestor, especially if you are researching an Irish convict because of the absence of court records. The main newspaper at the time in Ireland was the *The Public Register* or *Freeman's Journal.* Barbara Hall was able to discover quite a few of the crimes and convictions of the 1000 convicts transported to New South Wales in the 1790s. The *Belfast Newsletter* was another that proved fruitful and provided interesting reading.

Convict Bridget Eslin, who was transported along with her brother Patrick in 1793, came from a criminal family that the *Freeman's Journal* described in detail over the course of a few years. The Eslin family achieved notoriety around County Dublin for their involvement in stealing linen and calico from 'bleaching greens' from at least 1788 to 1792. Bridget's arrest was reported as follows:

> Mary Hughes and Bridget Eslin, for stealing out of a bleach-green at Rathgate, forty yards of linen, value 2 shillings, the goods of Mr Osboy. They were stopped loaded with the spoil by a revenue officer, who suspected that the bundle contained smuggled goods. Guilty to the value of 4/6d, transported for seven years.
>
> A singular instance these young women exhibited of the incorrigible perverseness of early depravity; the father

> of both was hanged, and the mother and brother of one of them was transported within the short space of two years, for similar offences.

It was Bridget's father Patrick who was hanged in 1789 for similar offences. Bridget's mother and brother John were sentenced to transportation to America at this time. Bridget arrived in New South Wales aboard the *Sugar Cane* in 1793 and eventually settled into a life on the land. Within three years of arrival she was living with an English convict, Robert Hobbs, who had arrived in 1791. They were together for at least 43 years until Robert's death in 1839, and had nine children together. Bridget died in 1843 aged about 69. We've met a few descendants of Bridget's at family history events, and it's estimated that there could be thousands of descendants.

The Irish Newspaper Archives (irishnewsarchive.com) and the British Newspaper Archive (britishnewspaperarchive.co.uk) are both paid subscription sites that offer searchable access to historical newspapers. Some newspaper archive sites, including those two, are also searchable for free to card holders of the National Library of Australia and state libraries via their eResources portal. Some access may be limited but it's a good way to start researching without the upfront price tag. In some instances you may only be able to access the eResources portal onsite at the relevant library.

The convict era is both fascinating and harrowing in equal measure. It's a rewarding one to research due to the wealth of information available and the insight this gives you of life at the time. Whether you discover a link to someone like highwayman Thomas Hyndes, First Nations businesswoman Maria Lock or career thief Bridget Eslin, it'll be well worth the effort.

CHAPTER 8

Immigration and shipping records

AT A GLANCE: *Knowing when and why your immigrant ancestor arrived in Australia gives context to their lives. Luckily, some immigration records still survive, and many are freely available online. We'll discuss where to look and what you can expect to find.*

'Everitt, John, 36, Blacksmith, Protestant,
could read & write, Limerick, bounty £19
Everitt, Ellen, 34, House Servant, Protestant,
could read & write, Limerick, bounty £19
Everitt, Edward Wm, 9, son, Protestant,
could read & write, Limerick, bounty £10
Everitt, Joseph, 4, son, Protestant, Limerick, bounty £5
Everitt, James, 11 months, son, Protestant, Limerick,
no bounty, under age
Everitt, Mary, 12½, daughter, Protestant,
could read & write, Limerick, bounty £10
Everitt, Sarah, 10, daughter, Protestant,
could read & write, Limerick, bounty £10'

Assisted immigrants digitised shipping lists 1828–1896, MHNSW

COMMON TERMS YOU'LL COME ACROSS

Assisted immigrant Someone whose journey to Australia was paid for (or subsidised) by someone other than themselves, such as via a government immigration scheme or employer. Someone who received an incentive (such as a land grant) to migrate was also often included in lists of assisted immigrants.

Bounty scheme The government specified the categories of migrants needed (including age, gender and occupation) and then paid someone (such as a colonist or a shipping company) who brought suitable migrants fitting those criteria to the colony.

Naturalisation The process of gaining the rights (such as to own land or to vote) of a citizen. Prior to 1949 in Australia, that meant obtaining the rights of a British citizen. (Those born in the British Empire were already British citizens.)

Passenger list A document recording passengers, and sometimes crew, on board a ship.

Shipping record A record that might be used to refer to ship arrivals – or it can more loosely refer to those who travelled on that ship. More often than not, a passenger list is the most useful to family historians.

Unassisted immigrant Someone who paid for their own passage to the colony. In some colonies, only those assisted by governments were included in the lists of assisted immigrants and all others appeared in the lists of unassisted immigrants.

When the Everitt family arrived in the port of Sydney on 20 October 1841, it's a fair assumption to say that the colonial government knew more about them than the Everitts knew about their new home. The information about the Everitts listed earlier can be found on the passenger list for the *Livingstone*, the ship on which they arrived to begin a new life in the colony.

It is the 10-year-old Sarah recorded on the passenger list for the *Livingstone* who is the great-great-grandmother of genealogist Kerry Farmer. And it's Kerry who uncovered Sarah's life in the colony. By working backwards (remember golden rule #1) from the information on Sarah's death certificate, Kerry was able to piece together her story from arrival on the *Livingstone* as a little girl accompanying her family to start a new life. Kerry is our expert who will walk us through the shipping records that are available in Australia. Knowing when and how your ancestors arrived in the country can answer a lot of questions and give you context as to why they migrated.

A big dose of curiosity is what sparked Kerry's investigations into her family history. 'I grew up surrounded by my mother's family, which had some complicated relationships, so I found myself asking questions. I didn't always get the same answers from the different people I asked!' explains Kerry. 'Later I attended a funeral of someone from my Dad's side and I didn't even know many of the people at the funeral and how they were related to me. When I asked, it seemed there were more complicated relationships – an adoption, divorce, changes of name. Some people I asked not only could not answer my questions, but also seemed content not knowing. So I found myself trying to build a family tree and find the answers that no one could tell me.'

Fast forward a few years and Kerry is now a presenter and teacher in genealogical studies, as well as a Fellow and

Director of the Society of Australian Genealogists. Kerry has written two books, including *DNA for Genealogists* (Unlock the Past, 2017) and *Arrivals in Australia from 1788* (Unlock the Past, 2015), so has extensive knowledge of shipping records and immigration patterns to Australia.

The bounty price listed after the Everitts' names was not because they were wanted criminals. Parents John and Ellen Everitt and their five offspring were immigrants, brought out to Australia via a 'bounty scheme'. This was an arrangement where the government specified the sort of migrants they wanted, and were prepared to sponsor them to come to Australia. The criteria generally included specifying age and occupation, says Kerry. 'A settler in the colony employed immigration agents in the UK to find suitable immigrants. The settler paid to bring out the migrants for which they were paid a bounty by the government. The bounty was more for men and women of a working age, and with an occupation that was in demand, and less for children.' In-demand occupations changed over time, says Kerry, but in the mid-19th century, for example, farm labourers and trades related to house construction were most sought after.

Bounty immigrants had to provide certain information and references before they could emigrate. In the Everitts' case, they needed to provide details of John and Ellen's parents, and their occupations. They were then judged on whether they were the sort of people that the colonial government was prepared to sponsor to set up camp in the new colony. It's possible that John and Ellen, in making their decision to move to the other side of the world, knew very little about their destination, other than it was where convicts were shipped to, and that it was heralded as the land of opportunity for those willing to take it on.

Migration to Australia has been happening for tens of thousands of years. It's not exactly certain when First Nations people arrived on the continent we now call Australia: some studies estimate it was 65 000 years ago, while genetic analysis by researchers in 2017 of historic Aboriginal hair samples, conducted with the permission of descendants, suggested that it was around 50 000 years ago. This same study showed that once migration began, populations spread around the east and west coasts of Australia.

But how did they get here? The same researchers surmised that they entered this great southern land via a landmass where New Guinea was connected to Australia, but only after hazardous voyages across open water in southeast Asia that would have taken much prior planning and maritime knowledge.

Those two factors also played their part in the European landings here from 1788. First there was the wave of convicts escorted by the authorities instructed to establish a new British colony. Then swathes of migrants from many different countries – those who arrived free like the Everitts – started to make Australia their new home. We've looked at convict arrivals separately in chapter 7, but here we'll be focusing on those who arrived as free immigrants during the 1800s and 1900s.

Most of us these days think of ourselves as global travellers. We book a plane ticket and travel to a far-flung destination to experience that country, to see family, perhaps to move there. It might surprise you, though, to learn that our ancestors did much the same thing, although the travel took somewhat longer. From the 1800s, people criss-crossed the globe in search of experiences, to build a new life, to escape an old one, and for work. For those with the funds to afford it, travel in and out of Australia was an option. But for the most part, those who migrated here, either couldn't afford the passage back, or chose not to return. Many records from this time survive, though with varying amounts of information contained in them, depending on who was keeping the records and why.

What are shipping records and what do they contain?

There can be a lot of information in shipping records, or there can be very little, depending on whether your ancestor was an assisted or unassisted migrant.

Between 1788 and 1830, migration to Australia was largely made up of convicts, the soldiers and government officials needed to manage a convict colony, or those British people who thought that the colony might offer opportunities that they otherwise wouldn't have had. The wool industry was thriving and land was being opened up on the other side of the Blue Mountains for colonists to perhaps make their fortune. But by the late 1820s both the British and colonial governments saw an opportunity to export a different kind of migrant to our shores – free migrants. It could solve two dilemmas in one – the widespread unemployment in Britain, and the lack of skilled labourers and single women in the colony, especially in the interior of the country where there was a lack of both. The original *Farmer Wants a Wife*, if you like.

It was a time when there was mass migration from Europe, but people were mostly emigrating to America and Canada, closer and cheaper options than Australia. To entice them away from this trans-Atlantic migration, the colony had to offer incentives to people to travel all the way to Australia, says Kerry Farmer. 'At various times governments offered cheaper fares or even land to the most desirable migrants – those who were of a suitable age or had a skill that was needed. Governments recorded details of the immigrants they sponsored, and many 19th- and 20th-century immigrants to Australia can be found in those lists of "assisted immigrants".'

The first assisted migrants arrived in Sydney in 1828, and the scheme grew from there to other colonies (and then states after Federation). When selecting migrants to sponsor, governments asked questions about both the migrating family, and sometimes, as we saw in the case of the Everitts, details of the migrants' parents. Typical information in a passenger list for an assisted migrant can (but does not always) include their name, age, occupation, religion, native place (place of birth, or last place of residence), literacy skills, intended employers, length of work assignment, wages or rations, and if the migrant went to work for their employers or left 'on own account'.

However, not all migrants received assistance towards their passage to the colonies. Many were 'unassisted' travellers, required to pay their own way. Escaping war and famine, or chasing the opportunity to strike it rich on the gold fields, lured many people to the colony. But there's a difficulty here for family historians. 'For the migrant who paid their own way (or their fares were paid by family, a charity or even a future employer), generally far less information was gathered', says Kerry. 'Many were not even named.' Prior to 1852, for example, the master of the ship was not required to record the names of unassisted passengers.

The way to search for both assisted and unassisted migrants is the same; it's just that you're more likely to get more information if your ancestor was assisted.

Where do I find passenger lists?

Generally speaking, passenger lists for arrivals prior to 1924 are held by each state archive (we'll cover how to search these later in the chapter). After this date, immigration records are held by the National Archives of Australia (NAA), when the Commonwealth Government took responsibility for all arrivals to Australia. The main exception to this is arrivals to the port of Fremantle in Western Australia, which opened in 1897. All records for arrivals in Fremantle are in the NAA databases.

However, before you start checking every state archive's shipping records, or indeed, the state archives in which your ancestor settled, you need to consider two things. First, you'll need an approximate date of when they might have arrived so you can narrow down your search. 'Use clues to be found in, for example, where and when their children were born, to get an idea of where and when they had arrived', says Kerry. Or in Sarah Everitt's case, information contained on a death certificate. More on that in a moment.

Second, you'll need an understanding of the shipping routes in the 1800s and 1900s. Why? Because wherever their first port of call in Australia was, that's where the records are likely held for that ship, even if your ancestors ended up travelling on to another area within Australia. 'You need to consider the route that people took to their final destination in order to know where to look for records of their arrival', says Kerry. 'Most people who came from Europe to Australia before the 1880s travelled on ships that followed the trade winds and took the "Great Circle Route" from Europe, south through the Atlantic Ocean, around Africa, and from there they travelled eastwards to Australia, most commonly stopping first in Sydney and/or Victoria.'

TOP TIP Passenger lists are usually held by the state where the ship first docked in Australia, even if that wasn't where your ancestor finally settled.

It's also well worth checking the shipping lists in newspapers in the relevant date range you're looking at. You can usually discover details of when the ship arrived into port, and sometimes names of those on board who travelled in the better modes of class. Kerry tells us, 'Newspapers' shipping lists often named arrivals, particularly for those who travelled in cabin class, and especially for intercontinental travellers. Some immigrants' arrival might only be included in the newspaper [as] "and 86 in steerage" – so you might never find them mentioned by name.'

'For immigrants arriving in South Australia, newspapers are often the best source for those names', says Kerry. 'This is because less than 15 per cent of 19th-century official lists of assisted immigrants arriving into South Australia have survived – and also many passengers travelling to South Australia were on ships that stopped first in Victoria.' A simple search on Trove (see chapter 9 for more) for your ancestor's name could yield a result, or search Trove more broadly for shipping news in the timeframe you're investigating.

So if you're looking for an ancestor who arrived prior to 1880, Kerry recommends looking in the Victorian or New South Wales government archives, or often both. From Melbourne (known as the Port Phillip District of NSW until 1851) or Sydney they may have travelled on to their final destination by land or by the coastal ships that travelled between the Australian ports, but as Kerry has mentioned, it's their arrival port which is most likely to hold the record of their immigration. Some ships travelled directly to Hobart, but it was more common to disembark in Victoria or New South Wales, then travel to Tasmania from there. 'There are far fewer records of those who travelled by this domestic [coastal] shipping [route], so it might be difficult to actually find a record of someone's arrival at their final destination', says Kerry.

'Although the Suez Canal opened in 1869, most ships at that time continued to use sail when possible, so it was not until the 1880s that the Mediterranean and Suez Canal route really became a viable alternative from Europe to Australia, allowing ships to steam through the Suez Canal, travel past Indonesia and southwards down the coast of Queensland.'

However, ships still commonly travelled the Great Circle Route, especially when the port of Fremantle opened in 1897. 'After that date most ships travelling around Africa and then on to Australia stopped first and completed their immigration record in Fremantle. Those records are best searched in the NAA', says Kerry.

'Most surviving passenger lists refer to those who took the Great Circle or Suez route from Europe to Australia, as these were the most common routes. There are few records of those who travelled from or via North America or maybe from India. There are also few records of those who travelled as crew, or in military regiments', says Kerry.

How do I find out when my ancestor arrived?

There's no one-stop shop when it comes to historical shipping records. Various government agencies and subscription sites have different information, so the best bet is to systematically work your way through them all, starting where you think you'll most likely find them, given the evidence you already have to hand.

Let's use Kerry's great-great-grandmother Sarah Everitt (sometimes spelt Everett) as an example. Sarah's death certificate in 1885 revealed crucial information, explains Kerry. 'It stated that she was aged 55, born in Ireland, and that her parents were John Everitt (a blacksmith) and Ellen Brummell. It also said that she had lived "40 years in NSW". Her son provided the information for her death certificate, and I can imagine that, when asked, "how long was she in New South Wales?", he might have thought, "oh, about 40 years". Always allow for these answers to be approximate – and that applies to approximate spelling too.'

Armed with this information, Kerry deduced that she was looking for a Sarah Everitt (or Everett) born about 1830 in Ireland, arriving in Australia sometime in the 1840s, if her son was correct in saying that Sarah had been in the colony for 40 years. It was something for Kerry to go on, a place to start in the records and see where the leads took her. And crucially, there was enough information about Sarah's parents to allow Kerry to crosscheck with other sources to make sure that when (or if) she found her, she'd know it was the *right* Sarah Everitt she was searching for.

Based on the information on Sarah's death certificate, Kerry started by searching the New South Wales passenger lists, given that Sarah lived most of her life in New South Wales and it was the most likely port for her disembarkation.

The NSW State Archives index to names of assisted passengers into Sydney starts from 1844. When that was unsuccessful, Kerry did a search on Ancestry in the 'Immigration & Travel' category of records for a 'Sarah Everitt' within the Australian

Collection focus. That also listed no one of about the right age. Next she searched for 'John Everitt' – and this produced 45 results – but only one of about the right date and mentioning that the John Everitt was from Limerick. That record was for a bounty immigrant who arrived on the ship *Livingston* in October 1841.

Looking in the 'Assisted immigrants digitised shipping lists 1828–1896' on the NSW State Archives website, that listed the 1841 ship name as *Livingstone* not *Livingston*. Kerry looked in the digitised lists of passengers – and bingo, she found the family arriving on the ship *Livingstone* in Sydney on 20 October 1841 – John, Ellen, Sarah and her four siblings, Edward, Joseph, James and Mary were all listed.

The digitised document also told Kerry that they were bounty immigrants – assisted immigrants worthy of being sponsored because the parents had skills the colony wanted and because the majority of the children were of an age where they would soon be able to work.

Armed with this crucial information, Kerry turned to FamilySearch, which lists an index called 'Australia, New South Wales, Index to Bounty Immigrants, 1828–1842' on its site. From here she garnered further crucial information: that Sarah's father, John Everitt (the blacksmith) was the son of another John Everitt (a nailer) and Ellen, and that Sarah's mother Ellen was the daughter of Edward Brummell (a nailer) and Susan. (Curiously, the FamilySearch index also listed the ship as the '*Livingston*', not '*Livingstone*' as on NSW State Archives.)

It was from this additional information that Kerry knew she had the right Sarah Everitt in the records. 'The names and occupations of Sarah's parents matched information on her death certificate and even provided additional information about Sarah's grandparents', Kerry says.

After confirming she had the right Sarah Everitt, Kerry's next step was to get more context about her ancestor beyond names in the records. The FamilySearch record also said that the family was brought out by Robert How and Company. By searching the *New South Wales Government Gazette* on Trove, Kerry learnt that Robert How and Company was a company of merchants.

By also searching Trove for shipping news in the newspapers, Kerry found a report in the *Sydney Morning Herald* dated 21 October 1841 of the ship's arrival into Sydney, noting that the *Livingstone* actually departed from Liverpool, England, on 28 June 1841. 'So the family from Ireland must have made their way to England to take the ship', says Kerry. And from the shipping news in the *Sydney Gazette* the same day, Kerry learnt that there were 232 migrants on the *Livingstone*, of which 228 were bounty immigrants.

Even though the Everitts were not named in the newspaper articles, all this additional information gave Kerry detail and context about Sarah's arrival in New South Wales.

Naturalisation records

A second important source for discovering when your ancestor might have arrived in Australia is naturalisation records.

As Kerry says, 'Prior to 1949, there was no concept of citizenship in Australia. You were either a British subject or citizen and therefore eligible to own land and vote, or you were "an alien", meaning from elsewhere in the world.' This, says Kerry, 'meant that anyone not born in the British Empire (for example, those who were born in the Americas, Europe, Asia and Africa) needed to be "naturalised" in order to get the same rights as citizens, including the right to own land and voting rights'.

'This means that these records are a great source of arrival information into Australia because as part of the application for naturalisation, people were asked where and when they were born and when they came to Australia, as well as the ship that brought them.'

'Sometimes people were naturalised many years after arriving in Australia, when they had saved up enough money to buy land and so needed to be naturalised', says Kerry. This can mean, though, that if it's many years since their arrival, their memory of information may have faded. 'I've seen a few interesting ones where perhaps somebody was naturalised 40 years after they arrived', says Kerry. 'And when they're asked for the name of the ship they sailed on, they have said they can't remember.'

Again, dates before and after Federation play a key part in where you can find naturalisation records. 'Before 1904, naturalisation was administered by the colonies or states', says Kerry. 'However, if someone was naturalised in one Australian colony and then moved to another, they had to be naturalised again in the new colony before they could own land. From 1904, naturalisation was handled by the Commonwealth Government, and once someone was naturalised once, the same rights applied anywhere else in Australia.'

Records of naturalisations after 1904 (as well as records of the Victorian and South Australian naturalisations prior to 1904) are held by the National Archives of Australia (NAA). Other states' naturalisations are held in the relevant state's government archives.

Amanda King-Hardie, the manager of Reference and Community Outreach Services at the NAA, says the two main types of citizenship records are naturalisation certificates and case files. The NAA holds duplicate copies of certificates issued between 1904 and early 1962, at which time the Immigration department stopped creating duplicate copies.

'The NAA's naturalisation case files generally give more detail than the certificate, and can include information such as application for citizenship, oath of allegiance and other correspondence. Sometimes they will provide further information about the migrant, including date of arrival in Australia, ship (or flight) travelled on, town and country of birth, names of other family members, education, profession, and address in Australia at the time of naturalisation.'

Post-war migration

For the purposes of family history research, post-war migration is generally considered to be the decades immediately following the Second World War. Before 1948, every passenger ship or aircraft captain provided a list of passengers on their vessel when they arrived. And from 1948, air travel passengers filled in their own cards. Passenger lists on ships continued until 1965, when cards completely replaced lists for both air and sea travel.

Amanda King-Hardie says the best place to start with any search at the NAA is with their collection database, RecordSearch, accessible from their homepage at naa.gov.au. 'Using RecordSearch, you can conduct keyword searches in the basic search screen using a surname only or full name, or you may prefer to use the NameSearch tab to narrow down your results by type of record. If you are looking for a passenger record, then the Passenger arrival tab in RecordSearch is your best avenue, with most arrivals between 1924 and 1972 searchable by name in the passenger index.

'When using the RecordSearch database, begin with broad searches first, then refine your search. If your keywords are too specific to begin with then you may miss results. You may also need to think outside the box – are there any other names they may have used? Are spelling errors a possibility?'

In addition to passenger lists and naturalisation files, Amanda says there are a number of other record sets that can be useful when researching someone who arrived in the post-war period. 'Migrant selection documents, for example, are the documents completed by or for migrants applying to migrate to Australia under one of the many assisted passage schemes that came into place after World War Two, including those for resettlement of refugees and displaced persons.'

'The Australian Government's role in sponsoring or assisting migrants prior to World War Two was limited to providing funding to state-run schemes. After World War Two, Australia encouraged immigration, motivated by a need to improve the security of the nation. The National Archives holds migrant selection documents dating from 1945.

'Migrant selection documents vary in the amount of detail they provide. Generally, they contain a range of personal details such as name, address, place and date of birth, gender, marital status and nationality. Other details may include physical description, occupation, education, proposed employment and names of other family members, as well as health checks and photographs.'

Migrant case files, says Amanda, are similar to migrant selection documents in that they include a person's application to migrate to Australia. 'However, while Migrant Selection Documents are for those who came via an assisted passage scheme, migrant case files were generally created for people applying as unassisted migrants, those nominated by employer sponsors or family members and so on. While there are some migrant case files as early as the 1940s, most migrant case files in our custody are from the 1970s onwards. These later migration records are often not listed on our database, so you may need to submit an inquiry to the National Archives for assistance.'

Alien registration records are another source which might be useful in this period, says Amanda. 'Between 1916 and 1926, and again between 1939 and 1971, immigrants to Australia who were not British subjects had restrictions placed on them in the interest of Australia's national security. These immigrants, or "aliens", had to be registered and report all changes of name, address, job or marital status.' Alien registration forms may include information on the ship and date of arrival, date and place of birth, occupation, marital status, a physical description or photograph, and addresses in Australia.

Migrant accommodation or centre records may hold details of your ancestor's post-war arrival. Between the 1940s and 1980s, says Amanda, some migrants who arrived in Australia went to migrant reception and training centres or hostels. 'There were migrant accommodation camps all over Australia; however, the records of most of the camps did not survive to be archived, beyond some policy and administrative files. The Migrant Reception and Training Centre in Bonegilla (Victoria), however, is one main exception to that, as the NAA has a large collection of registration cards from those who stayed at Bonegilla. These cards usually include a description and photograph.'

Migration from a non-English-speaking country

What happens if your ancestor's first language wasn't English? Does that mean you need to look up their anglicised name on RecordSearch? Amanda says that while files can certainly be under an anglicised name, they don't tend to see that too often with the migration or passenger records. 'But it does come up from time to time with Naturalisation or Alien Registration records. This is because a person may migrate to Australia under their original name, and then may change or shorten it once they have settled into their new community. This can make things tricky for research when a grandchild who always thought their grandfather's name was Harry and is unable to locate his immigration record finds out that his name was actually Haralambos!'

Amanda says that some of the other research issues that can commonly occur with all records, but are more common with records of people from non-English speaking backgrounds, are:

- Spelling errors – names may have been spelt incorrectly by immigration officers or the applicants themselves. For example. K may be incorrectly written as a C, or a vowel being written differently due to differences in language (E and I may be swapped).
- Migration paperwork mixing up surnames and given names – this is fairly common due to different naming conventions across cultures, such as Asian cultures.
- Some documents may be in the original language – languages other than English – and there's not always an available translation.
- Some files may have been originally created with only a 'main applicant's' name in the title, rather than the names

of all family members who migrated with them. This can make it difficult to find a record if you are conducting keyword searches using the name of a child, but the file is actually only titled under their father's name.

This is just a very brief overview of the NAA immigration records, says Amanda. 'Our website is a fantastic resource, with subject guides, fact sheets, information on beginning your research, even tips and tricks – so it's a great place to start.'

Kerry's tips for delving into shipping records

'Because immigration records are not all held in one place, sometimes you need to look in multiple places – and even then you might not be successful', says Kerry Farmer. Based on years of experience, Kerry has developed the following steps for discovering when your ancestor arrived in Australia.

1 Establish the earliest date you know they were in Australia, and where, by working backwards through their life. That gives you a clue as to where and when to look for them.

2 Consider the reason they travelled at that time – this might give you a clue as to where to look. Was it because they wanted to escape something in their home country? What was happening in Australia at that time? For example, many migrants came because of the gold rushes in Victoria and New South Wales in the 1850s, or in Western Australia in the 1890s. If they were unsuccessful in finding gold, they might have moved on to live somewhere else. What was your immigrant's occupation?

Was it one that was in demand in Australia at that time and so they might have been able to take advantage of a subsidised passage? You might be surprised to learn that female domestic servants were much in demand, and so there was always a need for young single women willing to work. If your ancestor was a soldier, did they come with their regiment? If they worked on ships, did they come as crew?

3 Look in the relevant government's archives – the NAA from 1924 (and also from 1898 for those who stopped first in Fremantle), and for earlier arrivals look in state government archives. If you don't find your ancestor in the records of one state, then also check the other states' archives.
4 Check Ancestry, Findmypast and FamilySearch immigration records. All have slightly different records.
5 Search Trove, looking in newspapers' shipping columns for announcements of ships' arrivals. Sometimes the articles will name first class and cabin passengers.

As we mentioned earlier, finding when and why your ancestor migrated to Australia can give you context about their lives, both here and in the country of origin, so it's an avenue worth pursuing.

State-by-state details

Most shipping or immigration records are held by the government archives that were administering immigration at a person's first port of call in Australia. Prior to the 1880s this was most likely to be Victoria or New South Wales, or occasionally Albany in Western Australia, Adelaide or Hobart. After that time, ships continued to stop first in Sydney or Melbourne, but also ports in Queensland. From 1897, many ships stopped at Fremantle first. Cassie's paternal grandparents, for instance, who migrated from London in 1922, stopped at Fremantle before travelling on to Sydney. The passenger list for their ship of arrival is held at the NAA. After 1924, the Commonwealth Government started administering immigration, and records from that time onwards for all states are held in the NAA. If you're unsure of the timeframe for your ancestor's arrival, there is no harm in searching all state archive records.

Kerry has this general advice when searching for your ancestor's arrival.

'The most important point is to gather in one place all the information you have found for an ancestor (whether that "one place" is an online database, computer software on your home computer or even just in a word processing file or spreadsheet). When you can see where and when they were living in "the old country" and where and when they first appeared in Australian records, even if you haven't found the record of their immigration, you can deduce when it must have occurred.

'There are periods in Australian history where passenger lists are not complete or have not survived, and for some ancestors, maybe all you will ever know is that it "must have occurred about then".

'Maybe one day you'll find another record that can fill in the gaps in your ancestors' life. Maybe a death record or obituary mentioned how long someone lived in Australia or maybe a new collection of records becomes available.

'Above all you want to really think about and cross-check the information from different records to ensure that all the evidence is consistent and that you haven't accidentally recorded information from two different people with a similar name.'

Shipping records in libraries and archives

Most state libraries, state archives and the national archives have online help guides and videos on researching shipping records. Some general links are listed below. And for more details on shipping and immigration records, see Kerry Farmer's comprehensive book, *Arrivals in Australia from 1788* (Unlock the Past, 2015).

National Archives of Australia

As mentioned previously, the NAA holds all immigration records from 1924 onwards. Visit naa.gov.au/explore-collection/immigration-and-citizenship for details. However (there is always a 'however' when it comes to family history), these dates are not definitive – see the summary below for details on some of the records available at each state archive.

New South Wales

NSW State Archives houses New South Wales arrivals from 1788 to 1923. Some record sets are also available on Ancestry, Findmypast and FamilySearch. For more comprehensive details and guides, visit the Museums of History NSW site at mhnsw.au/archive/subjects/immigration-and-shipping. The State Library of New South Wales also has a handy guide at sl.nsw.gov.au/shipping_passengers/getting_started.

Victoria

The Public Record Office Victoria (PROV) holds records of Victorian arrivals of assisted migrants from 1839 to 1871 and unassisted migrants from 1852 to 1923. After 1871, records of assisted migrants were not kept separately from those of unassisted migrants and so can be found in the unassisted passenger lists. They also hold Victorian coastal passenger lists from 1852 to 1923, as does Findmypast and FamilySearch. The State Library Victoria offers a guide to available resources at guides.slv.vic.gov.au/migration/getstarted.

Queensland

Queensland State Archives lists arrivals from 1848 to 1912 and has indexed them in alphabetical order, not date order, so that you can search on a surname even if you don't know the date of arrival. Visit data.qld.gov.au/dataset/assisted-immigration-1848-to-1912 to search the data set online.

Also, in the late 19th century in Queensland, many Pacific Islanders were working in the sugar cane fields. As Kerry explains in her book, *Arrivals in Australia from 1788* (p. 79):

> When the American Civil War ended, cotton prices returned to normal levels. Some Queensland cotton farms switched to growing sugar. In the 1890s more 'Kanakas' were brought to work in the sugar cane fields – many of them kidnapped or tricked into coming, under a process known as 'blackbirding'. Following Federation (1901) legislation declared that all Pacific Islanders still in Australia in 1906 were to be deported. For further information see the Queensland State Archives Guide 51, 'Australian South Sea Islander records'.

South Australia

State Records of South Australia has searchable passenger lists from 1845 to 1886 and 1888 to 1940. Not all have survived, especially for those before 1845, so shipping news columns in newspapers are worth checking too. Visit archives.sa.gov.au/finding-information/passenger-lists-1845-1940 to search the indexes online. The South Australian Maritime Museum has also compiled a database of some 328 000 names for the years 1836–1964 and is well worth a look. Visit passengers.history.sa.gov.au to search the database.

Tasmania

Prior to 1820, immigration to Tasmania was actively discouraged. The Libraries Tasmania website says that anyone wishing to settle '… needed a letter of recommendation from the Secretary of State unless they were a convict or involved in the penal system. Some people could not land in Van Diemen's Land because they did not have these papers'. In the early 1800s colonisation was largely due to the convict settlement that was established in 1803. Libraries Tasmania offers access to many online record sets including 'Free immigration 1803–1946' and 'Assisted immigrant ships 1832–1889'. Visit libraries.tas.gov.au/family-history/arrivals-immigration-and-departures for more details.

Ancestry's Library Edition has access to 'Tasmania, Australia passenger arrivals 1829–1957'.

Western Australia

FamilyHistoryWA (formerly Western Australian Genealogical Society) has indexed a number of arrival and departure lists held by both State Records Office of Western Australia and the NAA. These include more than 26 000 arrivals between 1839 and 1890, including convicts and guards, and an index into 430 000 arrivals between 1898 and 1925 from overseas and domestic ports. Visit their website at fhwa.org.au for more details and to search the databases, some of which are free to the public and some are available to FamilyHistoryWA members only. Some indexes are also available on Ancestry.

Northern Territory

As Kerry explains in her book, *Arrivals in Australia from 1788* (p. 96), migration to the Northern Territory was slow, because the climate was generally thought to be unsuitable for European migrants. This 'explains the absence of the assisted migration schemes to the Northern Territory before 1928. Most early European arrivals in the Territory came to Darwin from South Australia or other colonies'. Search for information about the Northern Territory Archives Service records at navigator.nt.gov.au. There are also some records on Findmypast and the NAA. For a PDF guide to Commonwealth Records for the Northern Territory, visit naa.gov.au/help-your-research/research-guides/commonwealth-government-records-about-northern-territory.

CHAPTER 9

Newspapers and gazettes

AT A GLANCE: *A wealth of information survives in newspapers and government publications. Even better, Australia is one of only a few countries where these records are available freely online through the brilliant resource that is Trove. These resources are an excellent cross-reference tool to validate other records and to discover more about the social fabric of Australia. We'll look at how to search the records, plus offer some advanced searching tips if your ancestor has a common name.*

> Arthur Edwin Dellit pleaded guilty at Darlinghurst Sessions on Thursday to a charge of having fraudulently misappropriated cheques for £5600, the property of the Tasmanian Government. Judge White remanded accused for sentence, and allowed him out on bail of £1000.
>
> *The Argus*, 26 August 1921

Seeing your ancestor's name in print for the first time can evoke different emotions. Whether it's on a certificate of marriage, a shipping record or a graveyard inscription, discovering that paper trail gives you a definitive, tangible link to them – confirming that yes, they did exist; they had a life, dreams and ambitions. It

COMMON TERMS YOU'LL COME ACROSS

Almanacs Contain information pertaining to a specific region at a specific time and usually record items of interest such as government directories, acts and laws, medical practitioners, military establishments, shipping information, schools, and contextual information such as postage rates and statistics.

Government gazettes Official publications from the Commonwealth, state or territory government that cover government appointments, registration, migration records, acts and regulations.

Optical character recognition (OCR) Software that converts digital documents, such as newspaper articles, into searchable text characters.

Voluntrove Someone who corrects OCR text on Trove. There are currently more than 70 000 voluntroves who log in to Trove and correct the text in scanned articles.

can also, as in the case of family researcher Alison Dellit, turn all your preconceived notions about your family on their head.

Alison is the Assistant Director-General of Collaboration at the National Library of Australia (NLA). Her main role is to head up Trove, an online resource and discovery database run by the NLA. If you haven't discovered Trove yet, then you're in for a real treat. What awaits you is, yes, a treasure trove of millions of records, all digitised and freely available. Trove has a number of searchable categories worth exploring: newspapers and gazettes, magazines and newsletters; images, maps and artefacts; research and reports; books and libraries; diaries, letters and archives; music, audio and video; people and organisations; and archived websites. For our purposes here, we're focusing on newspapers and gazettes.

By far the biggest drawcard for family historians, the digitised newspaper and government gazette collections date back to *The Sydney Gazette*, the first colonial newspaper, which launched in March 1803. Newspapers covering most regions of Australia are on Trove, as are Commonwealth and New South Wales government gazettes, which contain information around government appointments and employment notices, legislation and private notices such as bankruptcies. While there are many avenues on Trove for family historians to explore (such as the underutilised oral histories), it is the newspapers and gazettes that are the best starting point for those new to family history. And this is the case no matter the timeframe that you're researching, whether that is the early convict years or at a later period. You might find very little or nothing on an ancestor (especially a female ancestor), or you may find quite a few mentions, especially if they were a figure of note, such as a politician, or a local business owner who advertised their wares.

It was in one of these digitised newspapers that Alison discovered the secret life of her great-grandfather, Arthur Edwin Dellit. The family knew nothing of his criminal past; even Arthur's grandson (Alison's father) was in the dark. Imagine, then, Alison's surprise when she discovered numerous newspaper reports about her fraudulent forebear – uncovered while giving a live presentation about Trove to an NLA audience.

'In the very early days', Alison says, 'when we'd only just launched Trove in 2009, I was doing a demonstration to a group of academics. There is obviously a learning here about not doing live searches in front of an audience! Because what came back when I typed my great-grandfather's name into the search box on Trove was an article about him embezzling [funds from] the Tasmanian government. This information was not part of my family's story that had been handed down, and I was quite shocked. It really threw me. I got through the presentation and afterwards rang my father. And he said to me, "Oh, no, that's not right. That was some other Arthur Edwin Dellit. Living in Bellevue Hill". "I'm not sure that's true", I replied. "I think it's your grandfather."

'In the next two years, as my parents investigated the story, we discovered that, yes, Dad's grandfather had gone to gaol. In fact, he was in gaol for the early years of Dad's father's life. And that really influenced my father's view of his father. It caused him to re-examine a lot of his childhood, because none of them had known that this had happened to the family.'

Newspapers and government gazettes can lead to thrilling and sometimes unexpected discoveries in family history research and we're lucky in Australia to have more than 1000 publications, from 1803 to the 1950s, digitised and freely available thanks to the team behind Trove. That's millions of pages that are searchable at the tap of a button.

Now, this chapter may seem like one big advertisement for Trove and the NLA and, well, you'd be right to think so. That's because Trove really is such a wonderful resource, enabling you to access information on 14-plus billion items, all for *free*. Articles related to your ancestors that you might expect to find in newspapers could be birth, marriage or death notices, obituaries, crimes and trials, public service notices relating to them, such as a letter awaiting collection, and advertisements for a family business, to name a few. If we look at Cassie's family tree, we've found an advertisement for her 5x great-grandparents' bakehouse at the Rocks in 1803 (selling bread 'At a fair and equitable Price'), an auction of their belongings in 1809, and the wedding of her great-grandmother in Orange in 1907 (the bride 'wore a very pretty gown'), just to mention three instances. Any mentions that you find of your ancestor, no matter whether it's a big story or just a small mention, are meaningful and can give you more information about their lives.

There are also other resources that offer access to newspapers, which we'll cover in a moment, but Trove really is the best place to look. Put aside some time to explore it; you won't be disappointed.

How to sign up and search Trove

Let's get down to brass tacks. Start by going to the Trove home page at trove.nla.gov.au. Click on the 'sign up' button, which allows you to create a free membership account on Trove. It should be noted that you don't need to sign up or be logged in to search Trove, but the advantage of doing so means that you'll be able to create lists and save what you've found, add tags, make notes, and correct text in digitised newspapers. You can also add a bio about yourself and what/who you're researching. All of these functions can be set to public or private, depending on your preference. We'll discuss these functions further in a moment.

Now that you're logged in, let's start searching. You'll see a search bar at the top of the home page. Trove will search exactly what you enter, so if you're searching for an ancestor's name, start with the spelling most common to that person. But

DID YOU KNOW? It was common for a married woman to be only referred to by her husband's initials or name in a news story, rather than her own name.

do broaden it out with different spellings if you don't find anything at first. As you'll know by now, spelling of names varied enormously – Smith, Smyth, Smythe – so work through variations methodically in the search bar and think phonetically. If searching for a female ancestor, you may find it more fruitful to search for her husband or partner's name.

Using our example, typing in 'Arthur Edwin Dellit' into Trove returns 377 results in the Newspapers & Gazettes category. By looking further into the results, we can see that there are 315 results in newspapers, and 62 in gazettes. We can also refine the results by place (state), newspaper title, decade, category, date range, illustration and word count. Right away, without refining any of the results, we can see that Arthur Edwin Dellit was embroiled in a court case for fraud in 1921 and 1922.

TOP TIP Even though articles will probably be the first items you want to read, don't disregard results that are labelled as 'advertisements'. They are also worth checking, as you might find, as in Cassie's case, an ancestor advertising a family business. And sometimes family notices or articles have been categorised as advertisements, so it's worth checking every result that Trove retrieves, if you can.

ADVICE FROM A VOLUNTROVE

Some family historians don't just dabble in Trove, some are voluntroves. For the past decade or so, these volunteers have spent their time correcting millions of lines of digitised text on Trove.

To explain what this means, we need to go back a step to the digitisation process. When documents such as newspapers are digitised, it is done using a process called OCR. In Trove's case, the library engages teams to complete each stage of this complex process. First up, each page of each newspaper is zoned into separate articles. These articles are assigned a category, such as News, Family Notices, Advertisements and so on. OCR software then converts each article into searchable text characters. Once these files are ready, the titles, subtitles, authors and first four lines of text in the articles are rekeyed manually to achieve 99 per cent accuracy, and the library checks the scans and OCR conversion for quality assurance.

It is after this that voluntroves come into play. OCR has enabled mass digitisation of documents, but it doesn't always render characters correctly. So these correctors go into Trove and correct line after line of text so that it is more legible for family researchers. A few even go a step further and link family articles to records on Ancestry, not only expanding their own family trees, but allowing others to do the same. One superuser, John Warren, will correct entire newspapers at a time, working through those articles most relevant to historians. He's up to 8 million-plus lines of corrected text. John told *Inside History* magazine that he finds the work incredibly rewarding. 'I know the work I do is appreciated by others insofar as it assists them with their family research', he says. 'I also learn a lot about the people who helped build our country, and many of the articles, particularly the obituaries, are very moving.'

Here is John's advice for finding family members on Trove:

Open vs restricted searches John's maternal grandmother's name was Martyr, which is a difficult one to search for. This is when he uses double quote marks and restricts the search to "Mr G Martyr", for example, and searches New South Wales papers. But generally he does an open search to begin with, covering all newspapers.

Know your article type Many historic newspapers have an article titled 'Personal', and this covers all the news about people, whether it be illness, death, births or weddings. One of these articles might cover 20 to 30 of these topics, and be between 1500 to 2000 words in length. If you're looking for a specific birth, death or marriage, you can restrict the search to just 'Family Notices' or ask it to include 'Articles' as well. Next to each article type is a number in brackets, referring to the number of results in that category.

Read the advertisements In many cases, entries relevant to family history research can also be found under 'Advertisements' because the people setting up the categories missed them initially. This particularly applies to Funeral Notices and Legal Notices about probate.

Often you can follow a story to its conclusion, especially a noteworthy story such as fraud, because the newspapers would usually report numerous times on its progress. Returning to the Dellit example, we can read about Arthur Dellit's trial and conviction, as the newspapers covered both in August and September 1921, including his imprisonment for 12 months in Goulburn Gaol in New South Wales.

And this raises another important point. You may assume this trial about fraud against the Tasmanian government, conducted in New South Wales, might only be reported in newspapers from those two states. But it was also reported in Victorian, West Australian and Queensland newspapers, plus in a South Australian newspaper using the spelling 'Delitt'. So don't just think local when it comes to searching for articles. Keep your search as broad as you can in the first instance rather than narrowing your search to the local or main newspaper from the area that your ancestor was known to live. Newspapers often syndicated stories to other states, and it may be in only those papers where the story survives and has been digitised. Or you may find extra details in one newspaper that don't appear anywhere else. And don't forget that newspapers don't just report crime; you might find stories about your ancestor's birth, death, a sporting achievement, or even a tale about their social standing or interstate travel. Often descriptions of a couple's wedding day were published, especially in regional areas.

Tips for searching common names

Searching for common names can be difficult unless you restrict the search by enclosing the words in double quotes. Quote marks allow you to search a phrase rather than single words.

Say, for example, your ancestor's name is Elizabeth Winter. Entering those terms without quote marks gives approximately 740 000 results for anything with 'Elizabeth' and 'Winter' in the article. Searching this way includes references to anywhere the name Elizabeth appears, as well as stories about winter recipes, weather reports and so on. Searching on "Elizabeth Winter" in double quote marks, however, restricts the search to just over 900 results where both names appear together in an article, and is more likely to yield the results you are looking for. You can further restrict this search by limiting the date range, place, type of article and newspaper title. This last restriction can be helpful in narrowing the number of articles you need to read, but as outlined in Arthur Dellit's case, newspapers carried stories from around the country, so to begin with, try to do an open search covering all newspaper titles.

If your search terms aren't bringing up relevant records, then, as with other sources, you'll need to vary the spelling of both names – Elizabeth may be Eliza, or Betty; Winter may also be spelt Wynter. Work methodically through all variations that you can think of, or have come across in other records.

If you're searching for a name where you only have a surname, try using the 'near' search functionality with a title by adding the tilde symbol (~) and a number indicating how many words can separate it. This will return results where the keywords are found near each other, setting the 'distance' between your keywords. So, for example, say you want to find a funeral notice for an ancestor you know only as Mrs Smith. Typing "Mrs Smith"~2 into the search bar will yield results where Mrs and Smith are within two words of each other. We can see on Trove that this yields more than 3 million results – too many to read, we know. But from this you can narrow the date range to the decade when your Mrs Smith was known to have died, for example 1890–1899. Narrow the field again to 'Family Notices' and you're left with just over 3500 results. A lot less than 3 million to trawl through. Although hopefully you'll already know more about Mrs Smith from other documents to help your search.

You could also try this search tool with a place name or occupation. For example, typing Readford Orange~3 into Trove reveals 2000-odd search results of the surname Readford (one of Cassie's ancestor's names) where the town of Orange features within 3 words of the surname Readford. You could also limit the search by putting the terms into double quotation marks like so: "Readford Orange"~3 and that limits the results to 16 records. Either way, your best bet is to look at any results that are in the approximate date range, and start reading them!

The Trove website also has other tips and hints for using the site, including more advanced ways of searching. Click on 'Categories' and then 'Newspapers & Gazettes' to find out more.

Your next step, after finding newspaper documentation of your ancestor, is to cross-reference the details with other primary sources. Always fact-check what the story says with records such as birth, death and marriage certificates, court records and so on. That way you can be sure that what you've found is correct and is about your ancestor, as opposed to someone else's.

In Alison's case, it would be to check with the gaol description and entrance book for Goulburn Gaol, where Dellit was incarcerated. As we've mentioned in chapter 2, government records such as these are held by the state archives and, in this case, also accessible on Ancestry.

5 TOP TIPS FOR SEARCHING TROVE

Here are our top tips for searching newspapers and gazettes on Trove, compiled from our own experience and experts at NLA who we've chatted to over the years.

1 Start simple before using the advanced search functions. Head to the Trove home page - trove.nla.gov.au - and type in a search term, such as your ancestor's name with the most common spelling, and see what results you get. Look for any results that may be in the approximate date range you're researching. Familiarise yourself with a simple name search first before moving on to advanced searches. These advanced searches require you to limit the search range by date, name or article type, and can mean you over-think the query and miss important results.

2 Look up the more uncommon names first to have more chance of success early in your search. 'I would start with the more unusual surnames in your family, rather than starting with the Smiths, or the Browns', says Alison. 'If you can start by thinking about the more unique aspects of your family history, whether that is a place that is small and local or whether it's an unusual spelling, you'll have more luck.'

3 Think local, search global. Remember that newspapers often syndicated stories around the country, so don't just search the papers local to where your ancestor lived. Start with a search of all newspapers and narrow the field from there.

4 Titles of newspapers changed over time. So when searching newspapers, you may need to look at the title details pages

to see which other newspapers you need to look at to capture the whole publication. You may also find that there are gaps for some years. This is usually because either the newspaper was not published during the date range, or the master microfilm or issues from those years have not survived or are otherwise not available.

5 Use the list function. This enables you to 'favourite' records, articles and web pages all in one place, making it easier to organise and refer back to them. You can also connect with people who have similar lists (for example, on the same families you are researching), and tag and comment on others' lists. To start a list, you'll need to log into Trove first. Start a list, and collaborate with others to share your finds.

Making a list on Trove

Along with the search tool, Trove also offers the ability to save your searches, and collaborate with others via a function called Lists. As part of this function, it will also offer you the citation details.

There are three types of lists on Trove: private, public or collaborative. Private lists are visible only to the person who created them (the list owner). Public lists are visible to everyone. Only the list owner can edit them, but anyone can add tags and notes. Collaborative lists are also visible to everyone. The list owner can edit them, and so can people who have requested to join the list and have been approved by the owner. Anyone can add tags and notes to them.

To start a list, you'll first need to log in to Trove. Find a newspaper article that you want to add to a list, then in the sidebar menu on the left-hand side of the screen, select the Lists icon. Select the Add button, then the blue + button to create a new list. Enter a name for the new list (such as the family surname) in the 'Make a new list' field. Enter an optional list description – it's a good idea to do this so you remember what the list is about. Tick the relevant box indicating if you want the list to be private, public or collaborative. Note that your Trove profile needs to be public if you want to collaborate on a list. Hit the save button and voilà, you've made your first list. Now you can save articles of interest, and share what you've found with others.

And if Trove draws a blank and returns no results relevant to your ancestor? Don't feel dismayed. Find the newspaper local to where they lived, drill down into the date range of when they lived there, and start reading. It'll tell you so much about the social fabric of their community and what their daily lives were like, and will provide a window into the news and topics of conversation, just like newspapers do today. You'll discover more about how they lived, even if you can't find a specific article about them.

Trove speaks your ancestor's language

Trove is truly multilingual as well. It contains not only searchable newspapers published in English, but also those that were printed in other languages, including Chinese, Dutch, Estonian, French, German, Greek, Indonesian, Italian, Japanese, Macedonian, Polish, Portuguese and Tetum.

And it will search across all those languages for you, not

just English search terms. Type in a keyword in Aboriginal and/or Torres Strait Islander languages and non-English languages for results in that language. You can also enter the name of an Aboriginal and/or Torres Strait Islander language to see results that may contain the language.

Other newspaper resources

As we mentioned earlier, there are other newspaper resources you could investigate. State libraries and local libraries may have access to publications not yet on Trove, or from after 1954. Family history and local history societies may also have local newspaper archives.

The excellent eResources database, available to all NLA and state library card holders, is well worth a look. We've pointed to this in other chapters, and it's relevant here too. You'll find additional newspaper archives from around Australia and overseas. Just log in using your library card to the relevant library website and search on eResources. Read the handy research guide provided before you start.

What's next for Trove

Trove, as with any online collection, is an evolving resource. More and more content is being digitised and made accessible all the time, and the staff behind Trove are currently focused on meeting the needs of migrant and regional communities, says Alison. 'We've digitised around 1800 pages of migrant diaries, with another 2000 planned. And we have a huge project looking at Australia's almanac history. For those whose families lived outside of cities, almanacs are a very, very rich source of name-based information. So we have lots of great content coming through.'

Our general rule, as with most family history investigations, is to be prepared for what you might find. As Alison's case shows, you could discover something about an ancestor that you find challenging or confronting. For others, a newspaper search of an ancestor could reveal a talent for sport, or baking – maybe they won an award for something – that gives you more insight into their lives and interests. Perhaps, depending on your age, you might even want to search your own name on Trove! Family historian Kerin Wanstall did, and she discovered a photograph of herself as a two-year-old taken while she was out shopping with her family at a department store sale. It had been published in the local paper, but she didn't know it existed and her family had never mentioned it, so she had no idea it was there on Trove waiting to be found.

Be prepared to spend some solid time on Trove – it's a rabbit hole. 'We have had people blame us for missing dinner appointments, or not starting their journey somewhere because they've lost track of time while looking through Trove', says Alison. There are titbits everywhere that will give you a window into an era, such as this one that we discovered while searching for a mention of an ancestor in the *Sydney Gazette and New South Wales Advertiser* in May 1820:

> WANTED, a Man who understands Horses, can drive a Cart, and make himself generally useful in a Family without grumbling. Reference as to Character for Sobriety and Honesty will be required. Apply at No. 16, Hunter-street.

It bears no relevance to our family trees, but it gave us a chuckle. And as this example shows, searching an ancestor's address in Trove could yield results. If your family was living at 16 Hunter Street Sydney in 1820, then you know they were wealthy enough to have a horse and cart, and employ a man to look after both. And were particular about the personality of said man!

Alison's further advice is to look at the government gazettes as well as the newspapers in the search results. 'Those contain government appointments, registration, migration records, and so on. There's a whole wealth of things in the gazette that are worth searching for.' Newspapers and gazettes are one category on Trove, so one search will cover both publications.

And remember, Trove isn't just about newspapers and gazettes – although that is what the majority of Trove users look at. The site contains a wealth of other material, including photographs, maps, audio interviews and sheet music, and can even help you find a library that holds that elusive out-of-print local history book.

Family history discoveries can be powerful and can change your perceptions of your ancestors. 'They contextualise the family', Alison says. 'The experience of looking at a house that someone lived in, for example, and I've certainly had that, is quite significant. We often have a surprising number of people who will write to us at the NLA saying they've discovered that a grandparent had a second family. That's not as unusual as you would think. So that's something that I would point out to people when they talk about family history. Be prepared for what you may find. It's certainly not uncommon to discover that before we had things like the internet and constant connectivity, people were maintaining separate families. And that kind of discovery is often surprisingly quite rewarding for people.'

CHAPTER 10

Military records

AT A GLANCE: *We cover enlistments, awards, medical records and more; Australia is lucky to have so many military records still surviving to this day. We'll show you what's available and offer handy advice on how to decipher abbreviations, acronyms and military-speak.*

> Bullets were flying past in hundreds. My word they had me bewildered. My friend Stan Wilson and I on arriving at Rifle Villa saw the frightful result of war. Here wounded lying in dozens and dozens were arriving from the trenches in front. We picked up our patient from amongst these mangled human beings and carried him right back to the motor about 1½ miles along the road, but this time we took no notice of bullets or snipers.

Diary of Wilfred Allsop, Fromelles, 19 July 1916

Discovering a diary like this can give you quite a jolt. The simplicity of its unvarnished language unveils a potent account of the stark reality of war. Reading those words also transforms Wilfred Allsop – service number 6777 – from a silent entry in a bureaucratic military record into a living, breathing human being with longings, fears and emotions. It's his voice from the

COMMON TERMS YOU'LL COME ACROSS

AIF Australian Imperial Force

ANZAC Australian and New Zealand Army Corps

AWM Australian War Memorial

BEF British Expeditionary Force

DOW Died of wounds

DVA Department of Veterans' Affairs

KIA Killed in action

m/i Marched in

m/o Marched out

NAA National Archives of Australia

POW Prisoner of War

RTA Returned to Australia

Some of the ranks you might find

AB Able seaman

Capt Captain

Cmdr Commander

CO Commanding Officer

Col Colonel

Cpl Corporal

CPO Chief Petty Officer

FltLt Flight Lieutenant

Lt Lieutenant

Maj Major

PO Petty Officer

Pte Private

Sgt Sergeant

SqLdr Squadron Leader

For a more comprehensive list, we suggest you use the AWM's glossary on their website. This contains a comprehensive alphabetical list of most abbreviations and acronyms you will find. We also recommend finding a copy of Neil C Smith's helpful book, *Understanding Australian Military Speak*.

grave, telling you what life was like for him in one small corner of the battlefield at Fromelles, during the First World War. Imagine if this was your ancestor.

Perhaps you have found a diary or letters hidden away in a drawer; maybe a medal has come to light; or you just know of some family folklore that 'Grandad fought in The Great War'. However your journey to trace your ancestor's past begins, if he – or she – served in the Australian Defence Force, the good news is there is an excellent chance you will be able to discover their records.

We are very lucky in Australia because, unlike family historians in many other countries, we have online access to phenomenally detailed archive documents. Because the army is a whopping great bureaucracy, they have created an extensive file on every serving soldier – which is excellent news for any of us searching for an ancestor. Most of these personnel records have been digitised, so you can get access to them with just a click of a mouse – and for free!

But where to begin?

We have enlisted the support of Professor Peter Stanley, UNSW Canberra, as our expert in the art of navigating these voluminous military records. Peter is one of Australia's most prominent military historians. He's published over forty books, mostly devoted to Australian military history. He was formerly principal historian at the Australian War Memorial, where he worked from 1980 to 2007. He is also a patron of Family History ACT, so he understands family history research.

You might be surprised to learn that Peter believes you shouldn't ignore family folklore. 'You know, people often say, "I can't believe family stories"', says Peter. 'Well, maybe, maybe not. It's all questionable. It should be questioned. You might find it confirmed. You might find it completely refuted by the

TOP TIP Create a chronological list of everything you discover, and do it right from the beginning. It's all too easy to get carried away with what you have found, and ignore the 'boring' admin bit. Add everything new to your timeline as soon as you find it – in date order – and don't forget to cite your source, its location and how you found it.

A typical example might look like: name, rank, service number and unit at the top, then start your timeline with their date and place of enlistment, followed by dates showing their ship of embarkation; where they served; if they were promoted, wounded or killed; where they are buried; the ship if they returned to Australia; and their service or gallantry medals.

Having a timeline that is easy to read will alert you to possible discrepancies between different records. If the dates don't match you should be suspicious as you could have the wrong person, so, like a good detective, investigate further to identify the record that is the villain.

To stand the best chance of success when you begin scouring the various archives, pull together as much information beforehand about your ancestor as you can – the more you have, the easier your search will be. Start close to home by interviewing members of your family to gauge things – see our interview questions on page 14.

evidence you find. But there could often be a core of truth in it. I think it's really important for people to understand that as a researcher, you're not looking for information, you're looking for evidence. And because you typically deal with thousands of bits of evidence, you can become overwhelmed, so it's important to plan and organise. You need to start with chronology; history happens in time. So you need to have a chronological framework to start with, and work backwards.'

Using the National Archives of Australia (NAA)

There are two key framework resources to use when you are researching an ancestor with a military connection: the National Archives of Australia (NAA) and the Australian War Memorial (AWM). There are a number of other resources and archives you can use to find your military ancestor, which we'll cover in a moment.

But let's start with the NAA. Don't be put off when you first log on to the website. It can be bewildering to a novice – under each of the tabs at the top you will find dozens of options, including their own help guides. If you follow our step-by-step suggestions, you will steer your way through the maze; once you have got to grips with the process, you can always explore their collections further.

One of the most significant documents you will find in the NAA archives is your ancestor's military personnel file. Every recruit – whether a regular soldier or a volunteer – had to sign an attestation document: a formal record that they agreed to serve in the forces. The NAA's records date back to the Boer War in South Africa, 1899–1902, and include every conflict that Australia has been involved in up to the end of the Vietnam War in 1975. The NAA has digitised these personnel files in a number of different series, depending on which war or conflict they served in. In Wilfred Allsop's case, he served in the First World War; that series is called B2455. If he had been in the

Second World War, the series would be B883. Behind these seemingly ordinary numbers lies an extraordinary volume of evidence, as the title page of Allsop's attestation record shows.

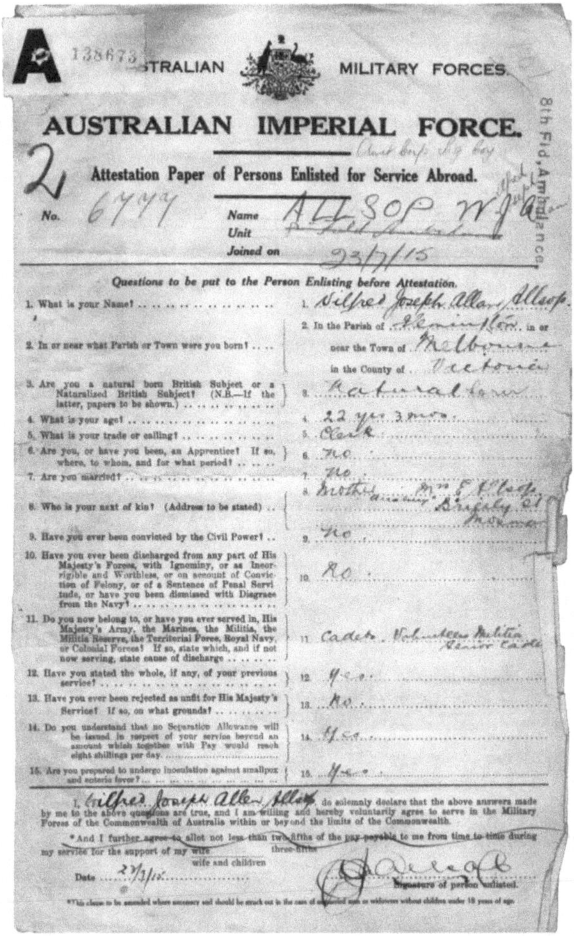

A 138673

AUSTRALIAN MILITARY FORCES.

8th Fld. Ambulance

AUSTRALIAN IMPERIAL FORCE.

2

Attestation Paper of Persons Enlisted for Service Abroad.

No. 6777 Name ALLSOP W J A
Unit
Joined on 23/7/15

Questions to be put to the Person Enlisting before Attestation.

1. What is your Name? — 1. Wilfred Joseph Allan Allsop.
2. In or near what Parish or Town were you born? — 2. In the Parish of Flemington in or near the Town of Melbourne in the County of Victoria
3. Are you a natural born British Subject or a Naturalized British Subject? (N.B.—If the latter, papers to be shown.) — 3. Natural born
4. What is your age? — 4. 22 yrs 3 mos.
5. What is your trade or calling? — 5. Clerk
6. Are you, or have you been, an Apprentice? If so, where, to whom, and for what period? — 6. No.
7. Are you married? — 7. No.
8. Who is your next of kin? (Address to be stated) — 8. Mother Mrs E Allsop
9. Have you ever been convicted by the Civil Power? — 9. No.
10. Have you ever been discharged from any part of His Majesty's Forces, with Ignominy, or as Incorrigible and Worthless, or on account of Conviction of Felony, or of a Sentence of Penal Servitude, or have you been dismissed with Disgrace from the Navy? — 10. No.
11. Do you now belong to, or have you ever served in, His Majesty's Army, the Marines, the Militia, the Militia Reserve, the Territorial Force, Royal Navy, or Colonial Forces? If so, state which, and if not now serving, state cause of discharge — 11. Cadets Volunteers Militia Senior Cadets
12. Have you stated the whole, if any, of your previous service? — 12. Yes.
13. Have you ever been rejected as unfit for His Majesty's Service? If so, on what grounds? — 13. No.
14. Do you understand that no Separation Allowance will be issued in respect of your service beyond an amount which together with Pay would reach eight shillings per day. — 14. Yes.
15. Are you prepared to undergo inoculation against smallpox and enteric fever? — 15. Yes.

I, Wilfred Joseph Allen Allsop do solemnly declare that the above answers made by me to the above questions are true, and I am willing and hereby voluntarily agree to serve in the Military Forces of the Commonwealth of Australia within or beyond the limits of the Commonwealth.

*And I further agree to allot not less than two-fifths of the pay payable to me from time to time during my service for the support of my wife / three-fifths / wife and children

Date 23/7/15

Signature of person enlisted.

*This clause to be amended where necessary and should be struck out in the case of unmarried men or widowers without children under 18 years of age.

Wilfred Allsop's attestation document dated 23rd July 1915.

SOURCE National Archives of Australia

Perhaps one of the more significant pieces of evidence you will find in these records is your ancestor's all-important service number. Every enlisted person had a service number which identified them and followed them throughout their service. Along with the service number, the personnel files will also note your ancestor's address when they enlisted; it will have entries about their physical appearance – things like birth marks or tattoos, as well as where they were posted and for how long.

It's a jackpot of information whether you're a novice or a superuser like Peter. 'I often talk about what I call framework sources or core sources', says Peter. 'So for example, I did a book called *Lost Boys of Anzac*, which is about the men who were the first wave who landed on Gallipoli, who died on 25 April 1915, and the core source for them was the AIF personnel files in the National Archives of Australia's Series B2455. And that was the absolute core because that was the beginning of trying to work out when these men died. And if they didn't die on 25 April, they were eliminated from the study.'

The best way to track down your ancestor's personnel file is to use the 'Record Search' function on the NAA website by typing naa.gov.au into your search engine. 'Record Search' is on their homepage under the tab 'Explore the Collection'. Click on 'Record Search' and it will take you to the main search page.

Using our diary extract example: select 'Name Search' from the tabs at the top of the main search page, and type 'Allsop' into the Family name box. Click the arrow on the 'Category of records' option. Select 'World War I'. Press search. And, hey presto, you get a list of 31 Allsops.

Ironically, if you knew Allsop's initials were WJA – but did not know the actual names – and you typed the initials into

TOP TIP If the spelling you have of your ancestor's name doesn't bear fruit, try as many variations as you can. Smith can be spelt Smyth or even Smythe; Williams can have one 'L' or two; and family names like Farquharson and Cholmondeley rely on accurate note-taking.

For example, if you type 'Loolong', the family name of First World War servicemen William and George, you get 'no records found'. But if you try 'Loo Long' you will discover their B2455s and an interesting story about George. He signed up twice. Rejected the first time for 'not being sufficiently developed', he tried again five months later, having found a less diligent examining doctor prepared to literally stretch a point: he made the grade.

the 'Given names' box on the main search page, you would get the dreaded message: 'No records match the search criteria'. The system does not like initials! If this happens to you, just try – as in our example – a surname and WWI or an even broader category like 'Australian Defence Forces personnel records'; it might create a long list, but by cross-referencing it with other information you have, you will succeed. It will just take a bit of perseverance.

If your search throws up more than one 'hit', it becomes a process of elimination – this is where your chronological list plays its starring role. When you have a list, as we do with our two pages naming 31 Allsops, you will see the column 'Item Title'. Each of the entries has the individual's full name; their SERN – service number; POB – place of birth; POE – place of enlistment (where they signed up); and NOK – next of kin. If you cross-reference information from your ancestor's birth certificate with the POB or NOK on the 'Item Title', you should be able to zero in on your ancestor's record quite easily.

You will also see a column entitled 'Digitised Item'. If there is an icon that looks like a sheaf of papers in this column it means you're in luck – the original paper records are available in electronic form, just a click away. If not, you can see the original by visiting the appropriate NAA viewing room. Although there are viewing rooms in each state capital, the record you want might be in another state's capital city, so you'll need to go there to view what you have found. If you can't do that, you can either request a copy online, for a fee, or engage a research agent – the NAA has a list of people and organisations that can be booked to do research on your behalf.

Policing the archive

The majority of personnel records have been digitised and are freely available as required by the *Archives Act 1983*.

But, as the NAA website explains, a small number of records are exempt from public use: 'Some are exempt, as defined in section 33 of the Act. Some personal information may require exemption for at least the lifetime of the individual. This can include medical histories, or details of personal relationships. A record may be withheld if its disclosure could adversely affect Australia's defence, security or international relations. This could include details of the design and construction of weapons, or records about intelligence-gathering, or information passed to the Australian Government in confidence by a foreign government.'

These restrictions apply to only a small minority of records: about 2 per cent of records are partially available; and a very small percentage – about 0.25 per cent – are fully withheld. So the vast majority of records are open and freely accessible.

One example of files that might be closed to public access is the collection of Repatriation files or Department of Veterans Affairs (DVA) case files. These are the files created by the DVA for veterans who have returned home and asked the DVA for help. Because much of this information is personally sensitive – things like details of their physical or mental health, the type of treatment they have received and their financial situation – the files are not always available for public access under the *Archives Act 1983*.

Although some records remain closed, many are open, so it is worth a search on the NAA website. You can retrieve records by using the 'Basic Search' tab on the Record Search page. Type in your ancestor's name and the word 'repatriation'.

Using our example again: Allsop's personnel file has been digitised and is freely available. As he served in the First World War, his records are in the series B2455. If your ancestor served in another war, you will find their personnel series number by choosing from the 'Category of records' option. The NAA has grouped the personnel records into four categories, found under 'Australian Defence Forces personnel records' in the NameSearch tab, to make the volume of records less cumbersome. The four categories are: Boer War; World War I; World War II; and Pre-World War I, Inter War and Post-World War II.

Once you have found your ancestor's personnel file, you will be able to track their every move throughout their time in uniform. You will know where they trained, what troopship they left Australia on, where they were stationed, any medals they were awarded and whether they were wounded or killed. It will give you a comprehensive account of their service.

The personnel files have numerous sections. Along with the personal details and medical clearance for when your ancestor joined up, you will also find a document entitled *Casualty – Active Service*. This is a diarised record of key events in your ancestor's service. It will show the date the entry was made, and from whom it was received. Quite often this will be the commanding officer or 'CO'. You will see things like the embarkation date and ship, arrival (or disembarkation, as it's referred to) date and port, any promotions, and whether he or she was ever admitted to hospital for illness or wounds. In short, it's a record of key events in your ancestor's military service.

You are also likely to find a page relating to *service medals* – every conflict or campaign had its respective service medal – usually denoted by a purple stamp. They will be signed, dated and numbered. If you have the actual medal, you should find your ancestor's name etched on the back or edge of the medal, along with their service number.

TOP TIP Be mindful of dates on Casualty forms. There are two dates on these forms: when the record was done and when the event actually occurred. Entries were done by clerks at Base Records in the order that they received the information, so that's the order that they are listed on the forms. The second column of dates records the date the event happened. If that information took longer to get back to Base Records, it could appear later in the list. So check the dates carefully.

Check, then check again

But before you add anything to your timeline, double-check it. This is particularly relevant to military records; unfortunately, that also includes details in the personnel files. Many AIF volunteers gave false details when they joined up. Perhaps the most common lie was giving their incorrect year of birth. According to the Australian War Memorial, in 1914 at the start of the First World War, the age range was 19–38 years, with a minimum height of 5 feet 6 inches and a chest measurement of 34 inches. In June 1915, the age range and minimum height requirements were changed to 18–45 years and 5 feet 2 inches. Many men fell outside of those age ranges, so they lied about how old they were so they would be allowed to join up. So double-check the military records with a birth certificate to make sure you have the right ancestor – especially if they have a common surname like Smith or Jones.

A trickier problem is if volunteers gave false names. One reason for this, as Peter explains, is that 'men often enlisted under assumed names, aliases, because they didn't want to be found. Remember, divorce, for example, was very, very difficult in 1914. And so lots of men enlisted under a false name in order to get away from marriages that they just wanted to bail out of. So they didn't want to be found'.

If this applies to your ancestor, help is already at hand in the form of some exhaustive work done by a former army officer, Neil C Smith. His book *What's in a Name* lists hundreds of aliases that soldiers used. You may be able to order a copy through your local library or the National Library of Australia.

The personnel records also contain another key piece of evidence – the next of kin. As Peter points out, that entry is so much more than just a name.

> **DID YOU KNOW?** There's a bit of mythology around the world wars that young boys would lie about their age in order to enlist. But by and large, that's not the case, says Peter Stanley. 'Most men in both world wars who changed their age actually put it down', Peter explains. 'It was much more common for an older man to claim to be younger than for a younger boy or a teenager to claim to be older.'

'On every man's personnel record it says next of kin, and that's a clue that this man enlisted from a family and that family was thinking about him right through the war. I had a terrible example for a book I did years ago, in which the son enlisted, and that seemed to be the biggest event in the family's life. And when I looked into the next of kin story for him, I realised that his sister died in the course of the war, of disease. His father became mentally ill, his mother was left destitute, and you think this man's service in the First World War was the most horrible thing that happened to this family?

'So take those steps to build up to know who you're working with, and start following a chronological story so that you can fit those pieces into the jigsaw.'

In their own words

As Wilfred Allsop's diary extract shows, knowing he was at Fromelles as a stretcher bearer is only one side of the story; it's when you hear his thoughts as he speaks to you in his own words that you truly begin to understand his life.

TOP TIP To give yourself a fighting chance of finding your ancestor's diary, try the state libraries first – their databases are easy to search online. If that doesn't bear fruit, select the most likely local town using their last known address and search the service clubs and the local library and museum.

Many of you won't have an ancestor's diary to hand, so it will take a bit more digging to discover if they kept one – and there are many to be found. The trouble is they have been donated to a variety of different institutions. The Returned and Services League of Australia (RSL) and the Australian Legion of ex-servicemen's clubs, as well as local and state libraries, museums and archives all have diaries in their care – Wilfred Allsop's diary is in the State Library of NSW's collection. Navigating the archives of multiple institutions can be a time-consuming and laborious effort but it will be oh-so-rewarding if you discover the words of your forebears in a handwritten wartime diary!

But even after exhausting all the options, and perhaps your patience too, you think it is unlikely that your ancestor did keep a diary, all is not lost.

Navigating the Australian War Memorial (AWM) collection

You can still get a feel for what your ancestor endured during their war service with the help of another key repository of sources – the AWM.

If your ancestor was among those who died in uniform, you are likely to find their name listed on the AWM's Roll of Honour. The record will also show their date, place and cause of death and their unit, along with the cemetery where they are buried. Your ancestor might appear on a memorial because their body was never recovered and there is no known grave for them. If you are looking at a First World War record, you should also find a circular completed by the deceased's next of kin asking for information about your ancestor.

You should also search the indexes to AWM 28 for any gallantry awards. Look for the official recommendation for the medal, as it will tell you why they were being put forward for a medal.

There are some other record series that you might find you can use to fill in any blanks you have or you can use to corroborate what you have found. One of these on the AWM website is the *Embarkation Roll*, AWM 8, which is a list of AIF personnel who left Australian shores to serve overseas. Along with the date they embarked, the port and name of the ship they left on, the record shows their age, occupation, where they lived and their next of kin.

The AWM also has another set of First World War records called the *Nominal Roll*. This is a list of AIF personnel who served abroad. Along with your ancestor's name, rank and service number, you will see one of three acronyms: RTA – returned to Australia, KIA – killed in action and DOW – died of wounds. If you are searching for an ancestor who served during the Second World War, you should use the Department of Veterans' Affairs (DVA) website. Their list of nominal rolls runs from the Second World War to the First Gulf War.

Indigenous records

If you are researching an ancestor with Aboriginal or Torres Strait Islander heritage, we urge you to search the various military records too, as many First Nations peoples answered the call to join up for military service. Recognising the potential sensitivities associated with these records, the AWM has a section called Indigenous Service explaining their position. We have copied it here:

> Background
>
> For the purposes of this list, the term Indigenous is understood as referring to the Indigenous peoples of territories administered and/or occupied by Australian forces: Aboriginal, Torres Strait Islanders, South Sea islanders and Papuans.
>
> The inclusion of words, terms or descriptions from historical records reflects the social and political attitudes of the period in which they were written. The memorial apologises for any distress that may occur.
>
> All reasonable care has been taken in compiling this information; details have been taken from publicly available records, including state and national archives, newspaper articles, genealogical material, family memorabilia, and oral histories. Discrepancies may exist; readers are strongly encouraged to contact the memorial if they have information that may improve the accuracy and completeness of the list.

Records from the front line

Part of the AWM substantial collection is the War Diary series. These documents are the official record that every unit had to keep while they were on active service. They catalogue every aspect of the unit's daily activities. They are an invaluable source that will fill in the blanks of your ancestor's military service, adding context to the personal data. The AWM also has a collection of personal diaries – if they are written by someone from the same unit as your ancestor's, you will get a personal account of their war service.

This is when thinking laterally again comes in handy. As Peter puts it, 'You need to look beyond the records in which they're named. So, for example, if you're looking at a private, that private may not be named anywhere in the battalion war diary, but the battalion war diary will document what their unit did, and their experience through the whole war. So I think it's important to look at the contextual records as historians, so you can get a bigger picture.'

Each war diary covers a calendar month, with a daily summary of activities and notes in the margin identifying appendices. These supporting documents are at the end of the diary and include despatches, orders and decisions taken, telegrams, daily situation reports, casualties, troop movements, enemy positions and accounts of operations. All in all, they are another illuminating source that will allow you to visualise and understand what your ancestor experienced.

Luckily for researchers, the War Diaries have been digitised and are easily searchable online on the AWM website – again, for free. You can even download a PDF document of the diary you find so you can refer to it later.

TOP TIP Remember that before you can search the War Diaries you will need the unit your ancestor served with. Your ancestor's personnel record will detail what unit he, or she, served in. But read all the paperwork as their unit might have changed during the course of the war.

You can find all of the War Diaries on the AWM website, under 'Collections' on their homepage. Right at the top of the drop-down menu you will see 'Official Histories and Unit Diaries' and then you will find 'Unit and Commanders' War Diaries' once you get to the next page.

Select the war they served in and you will get a list of all the main divisions – or categories – the AWM uses to group the various units together. In Wilfred Allsop's case, at Fromelles he served in the 15th Australian Field Ambulance unit. His unit's diaries can be found under the category heading 'Medical, Dental and Nursing'. In this case you will find quite a lengthy list, with the unit diaries for the 15th Australian Field Ambulance two-thirds of the way through. The AWM has arranged all the units' diaries in a month-by-month order.

When you track down the War Diary you are looking for, you will find they are written in two languages – English, and military speak! Your search could throw up entries like: 'Attack on German lines expected to take place. ADMS 2nd ANZAC visited. DMS 2nd ANZAC inspected MDS'. Most of it reads like gobbledegook. But translated it reads: 'The Assistant Director of Medical Services of the 2nd ANZAC corps visited. The Director of Medical Services of 2nd ANZAC corps inspected the Main Dressing Station'. It would be reasonable to interpret this as a top brass visit of medical facilities to see if they were up to the task, ahead of the expected casualties from an attack on enemy lines. It could be a significant moment in your ancestor's life.

Before we move on from the War Diaries, it is well worth mentioning the work of the acclaimed writer Charles Bean. When war broke out in 1914 the Australian government appointed him, via a poll of his journalist peers, as an official war correspondent. His dispatches were published in multiple Australian newspapers. In 1919 he became Australia's official historian of the First World War. His eyewitness accounts, often from the front line, combined factual notes of what he witnessed with his personal reactions to the horrors of war. If your ancestor was also in any of the battles that Bean wrote about, you will get an eloquent account of what they went through.

Luckily, Bean's diaries are also part of the AWM collection and, like the War Diaries, they too have been digitised. But they can be difficult to find, and hard to navigate. Peter Stanley suggests you seek out the published versions instead: *Bean's Gallipoli* edited by Kevin Fewster, and *The Western Front Diaries of Charles Bean* edited by Peter Burness.

However, if you remain keen to have a crack yourself, you will find them on the AWM website, under 'Collections'. When you select 'Official Histories and Unit Diaries' from the drop-down menu you will find 'Records of Charles Bean' on the next page. They are in chronological order, a month at a time. Bean's notebooks and diaries also hold more than just his thoughts on what he has witnessed. There are sketches of troop movements, maps of enemy positions and drawings of planned actions. That combination is a comprehensive and meticulous record of his time on the front lines, giving us a fascinating, often harrowing, first-hand account of every aspect of being at war.

Stories based on Bean's work were published extensively in the Australian press during the First World War. For families waiting anxiously for news about their loved ones, the national and local newspapers were often their only source of information. The National Library of Australia's Trove database is the best place to research newspapers – see chapter 9 for details on how to consult its database. Along with the stories from overseas, these same newspapers also include reports about troopship movements, especially the ships returning the wounded. Individual servicemen and women were rarely mentioned by name, but if you know your relative was on a particular ship, you may well find an account of the journey or background about the passenger list. Local newspapers also routinely published details, and sometimes stories, about those who had been wounded, or were missing or killed in action. You might also find they printed soldiers' letters to their families, despite the existence of the censorship regulations, as the authorities concentrated on enforcing those rules on major newspapers and in capital cities. So spending some time diving into Trove's huge pool of material will be well worth the effort.

Use with caution

There's a shortcut you could use, but it's one that comes with a warning.

You could sign up to commercial genealogy sites as we've described in chapter 2. Once you have signed up, you get access to their archives as well as the work of other members of the public who have uploaded their own genealogy research. On the surface that seems a very helpful concept. They could have data on your ancestor or another branch of his or her family

TOP TIP It's hugely satisfying to find that missing piece in your ancestor's past, but don't be tempted to ignore double-checking its authenticity just because it seems a good fit. It's far better to discover it's not your ancestor early on, rather than waste a lot of time – and emotional energy – by following the wrong lead.

tree, and it could save you weeks or even months of research – or maybe not. What if their finds are flawed? Have they been diligent in corroborating what they have found? Read it all and, as always, cross-reference and notate and cite everything you find.

Remember also, folklore should be questioned, says Peter. 'You might find it confirmed. You might find it completely refuted by the evidence you find. But there could often be a core of truth in it.'

Peter's advice about family folklore also applies to all research, including genealogy sites, and Google and Wikipedia searches. Turn information into evidence by double-checking everything with primary sources.

Additional sources

If you discover your ancestor was killed in either of the world wars, you can find their memorial site on the Commonwealth War Graves Commission's website: cwgc.org. It holds more than 1.7 million records commemorating the war dead. A simple search by name should find their memorial site or burial ground.

The International Red Cross archives house records of prisoners of war (POWs). Their website, icrc.org, has a searchable database for the First and Second World War POWs.

If you have a question about the First World War, there is a wonderful helpline in the form of The Great War Forum: greatwarforum.org. Once you have registered you can post questions to the group. They have over 30 000 members, so the likelihood of someone being able to help you out is high.

Perhaps your ancestor was at Gallipoli? If so, there is an association that is dedicated to that campaign: gallipoli-association.org.

If you can't find your ancestor's military records in the Australian archives, he or she might have signed up in another country. If they joined British forces, your best bet to find them will be The National Archives in the UK – discovery.nationalarchives.gov.uk – for personnel records and The Imperial War Museum (IWM) – iwm.org.uk – for private papers and photographs. For New Zealand, try archives.govt.nz and for Canada, search library-archives.canada.ca

Some expert advice

Our final food for thought comes from Peter Stanley. 'What I think is really important for Australian family historians is not to fall for the ANZAC legend. The ANZAC legend tells us that all Australians are ANZAC heroes. Well, I wrote a whole book called *Bad Characters* that really showed that some of them were heroes, and some of them were villains, and some of them were the same people. So for example, if you look at First World War personnel files, there are pages in their folios that talk about illnesses and injuries, and you'll find where they were wounded if they were wounded, but you'll also find out if they got VD. And you have got to accept that these are real people having experiences that we will never have, thank goodness. So seeing that military experience in perspective and remembering that sense of perspective is really important when you find yourself looking at things that you didn't expect to find.

'Do not censor it. History is only that if you tell the truth. If you sugarcoat it, or if you omit the nasty bits, or if you somehow emphasise the good and diminish the bad, you're not fooling anybody, except yourself. Although maybe you'll be fooling your grandchildren and you owe it to them to tell them the truth.'

CHAPTER 11

Who's in your DNA?

AT A GLANCE: *One of the biggest draw cards to family history in recent years has been the ability to take a DNA test and make a match with someone in the next street or half a world away who shares your DNA. It has revolutionised genealogy. We discuss the science behind the test kits and why it's a valuable tool for any family historian.*

> 'It was amazing. I watched this young woman become someone else entirely, simply because she discovered family she did not know existed. You know, for me, that's the power of DNA. It has this ability to reconnect us, to mend broken branches of the family tree.'
>
> Brad Argent, Head of Ancestry Studios

Since the start of the new millennium, millions of family historians have done a DNA test, and added science to our search tools in the quest to find those 'missing' ancestors.

As Ancestry's Brad Argent says: 'Ancestry's database alone is over 25 million, so I'd estimate the total global pool of people who have taken DNA tests is approaching 50 million'.

It's become so popular in recent years that, while writing this book, we had to think hard about where to actually put this chapter. For many, doing a DNA test is the initial jumping-off point for family history – it's transformational. It can instantly open doors to connect with people with whom you have shared ancestry. For others, though, it's a tool to confirm or refute research already done, or to break down brick walls when all other leads are dead (no pun intended). There's no right or wrong time to do a DNA test – it's completely up to you. But there are a few things to consider before you jump into the gene pool, which we'll run through here.

Ancestry's Brad Argent believes DNA testing is popular because it's so easy to do – you don't even need to leave your home.

'I think for a lot of people now it's their starting point for family history. It's kind of cool and a bit sexy because it's science and you get back a set of detailed results. You spit into a little tube, pop that in the post and off it goes. It gets to the lab and they extract your DNA from that – they don't do full genome sequencing, where they look at your entire genome. They just look at a bit of it, a relatively small bit of it. But we know that the bits that they look at are the bits that help us understand two key things. It gives you your ethnicity, and how you are connected to other people in the Ancestry database, matching you with other members of [your] family. We call it cousin matching.'

Who would have thought that spitting into a tube could connect you with family you never knew existed? But that's all it takes.

It's a simple two-stage process: do your DNA test and get your report, and then compare your test results with those on one – or all – of the various genealogy website databases. With the latter in mind, it's best to choose the company with the largest database. The bigger the database, the more likely

COMMON TERMS YOU'LL COME ACROSS

Autosomal DNA This test looks at the first 22 pairs of your chromosomes – your autosomes. It doesn't look at the 23rd chromosome; that is, the gender chromosome (X and Y). An autosomal DNA test can go back five to six generations, which is about 150–200 years.

'Cousin' matching When analysing DNA results, the company you've tested with will check if anyone else in their database has a match with your DNA result and highlight your relationship with them. It's often referred to as cousin matching, as the majority of matches are at that level.

Ethnicity report A report estimating what percentage of your DNA comes from which regions around the world.

mtDNA This is a mitochondrial DNA test that tests the female line (the X chromosome). Both males and females carry their mother's mtDNA, but only women will pass that mtDNA down to the next generation. It changes little from generation to generation, meaning that you can go back much further than an autosomal test.

Variant A change in DNA from one generation to the next. These variants allow us to compare our list of variants with other people's DNA registered on databases.

Y-DNA This tests the Y chromosome in the male line. Only men can take a Y-DNA test because only men have the Y chromosome, inherited only from their father. This test is helpful to confirm a paternal relation, or if two men with the same surname are related. Similar to mtDNA, Y-DNA changes slowly over time, meaning you can go back much further than an autosomal test to check a shared ancestral link.

you'll get a match. Currently, that's Ancestry, at nearly double the database of their nearest competitor, 23andMe. Then there is Family Tree DNA, MyHeritage and LivingDNA, who all have databases too.

Because you are relying on someone else to have taken a DNA test that is a potential match with yours, you may need to compare your results with more than one database. If that's the case you will need to download your raw DNA files and then upload them to another site. All of the aforementioned companies allow you to download your DNA but, currently, only Family Tree DNA, MyHeritage and LivingDNA let you upload your files to their sites, and for free. It's a clever way of expanding your possible 'hits' without going to the expense of doing multiple DNA tests.

The science behind the science

Knowledge about DNA, the building blocks of life, has come a long way since the 1950s when James Watson and Francis Crick, with contributions from Rosalind Franklin and Maurice Wilkins, discovered DNA's double helix structure. By the 1980s, labs were using DNA matching in paternity cases, and in the UK in 1986, DNA was used as genetic evidence in a murder trial for the first time. Police were investigating the rape and murder of two young women and decided to use a new technique developed by Alec Jeffreys and his team, from the University of Leicester. They had created a technique that could identify a unique DNA 'fingerprint' from a DNA sample. It was instrumental in the conviction of Colin Pitchfork. At the turn of the new millennium, DNA testing moved into the public arena. Nowadays, DNA tests are available – for a fee – to anyone who wants to research their family history.

DNA testing is a powerful tool because it can 'read' our genetic make-up. DNA is found in each of our cells and passed on from one generation to the next. The numbers relating to this biological data are staggering. A peer-reviewed article published by the National Academy of Sciences established that an average female has 26 trillion cells in their body and an average male has 36 trillion. Each of those cells, whether they are found in a saliva sample, a cheek swab or a blood specimen, contain the DNA that is our unique genetic blueprint – a sort of human barcode. If the barcode from your sample is similar to someone else's in one of the many genealogy databases, you've found a common ancestor. But how does the science behind a DNA test work?

The barcode in each cell of our bodies is made up of DNA which comprises 23 pairs of chromosomes arranged on what looks like a twisted ladder. DNA gets passed down from parents to their offspring through the generations – you get half of your DNA from each parent. Each time a child is conceived, very small changes, or variants, in the make-up of the DNA can occur. It's these variants in our DNA that allow us to compare our list of variants with other people's DNA registered on databases. The more you can match with someone else's, the closer your connection to them will be.

For those who discover a family member they didn't know they had, it can be a life-changing experience, as Ancestry's Brad Argent explains.

'We were filming a bunch of ads [for Ancestry] with a woman – let's just say her name is Charlotte. She was 27 and the only child of quite elderly parents – it's just the three of them. But as part of the process of filming, we did a DNA test and I was telling her off camera, "Oh, we have your DNA results back. And one of your cousins is trying to reach out to you".

'And she just went, "What?"

'So I explained, "You have a second cousin who's matched with you on the database and wants to talk to you".

'And it was amazing. I watched this young woman become someone else entirely, simply because she discovered family she didn't know existed. She said she was terrified of being alone. She said, "My parents are elderly. And when they're gone, I'm going to be by myself … and you're telling me I have family". It was obviously quite an emotional moment. But for me it kind of made me realise just how powerful DNA can be.'

The bit of science you need

Before you sign up to one of the companies offering DNA testing, you will need to decide which of the three commonly available tests is the right one for you, because they all do a different job. The three types of DNA test to think about are: autosomal, Y-DNA and mitochondrial DNA (mtDNA). It might seem that you need a science degree to choose which one to take, but you don't! As long as you know what each one does, you don't need to delve any further into the detail if you don't want to.

Of the 23 pairs of chromosomes in our DNA, only one of them determines our biological sex – the X and Y chromosomes. Females have two X chromosomes; males have an X and a Y. The other 22 pairs determine all our other features like our hair and eye colour, blood group and so on. These 22 pairs are known collectively as autosomes. (Please note that we are using 'male' and 'female' to refer only to chromosomal sex, rather than gender identity.)

Whichever test you choose, you will get a report. This will be in two parts: a map of your ethnicity – which parts of the world you have links with – and, if anyone else in the database has a match with your DNA result, it will highlight your relationship with them. The latter is often referred to as cousin matching, as the majority of matches are at that level.

So which test is best?

An autosomal test is the most popular because everyone has autosomal chromosomes, so people of any gender can take an autosomal DNA test. All of the main genealogy sites offer this type of DNA testing.

If you're tracing your patrilineal ancestry – your male line – you will need to use the Y-DNA test, because only males have the Y chromosome. If you're female and want to trace the paternal side of your family, you will need to ask a brother, father or grandfather to do the test on your behalf.

If it's the maternal side of your family tree you want to trace, the test to do is mtDNA – mitochondrial DNA. Although mitochondria are found in both the male and female sides of the family, they are only passed from mother to daughter. Because we all have mitochondria in our cells, any gender can take the test, but the results will only give you the female side of your family tree.

There are pros and cons to each of them. A big plus with autosomal tests is anyone can do them. But each time autosomal DNA gets passed down from one generation to the next, it undergoes a number of changes in its structure, so the further you go back, the less DNA you will have in common with your ancestors, limiting how far back you can go. But you can expect to get meaningful results in up to five or six generations. Both Y-DNA and mtDNA tests allow you to go back much further because the DNA passed down between the generations changes less than the autosomal DNA, but you will need to do both tests to cover the paternal and maternal sides of your family tree.

For the majority of people, the autosomal test gives them enough detail to potentially track down those elusive members of their family trees. However, you could opt to do additional tests if the autosomal one doesn't give you the results you were after, or if you want to narrow down potential cousin matches and shared ancestors.

An added extra – for free

You could also consider a company called GEDmatch. They were set up to overcome the problem of doing multiple tests and comparing the results with multiple databases in different companies. GEDmatch allows uploads from all of the DNA-testing companies and uses additional tools to drill down into your DNA in more detail – all for free. The only snag is that in order to match you with your other ancestors, they too need to

> **DID YOU KNOW?** A DNA test can not only potentially match you with relatives, but it can also indicate ethnic origins that perhaps you didn't know about.

have uploaded their data to GEDmatch. But many are doing just that, so you never know what you might discover. Visit gedmatch.com for details.

I have my DNA results, now what?

Getting your results can be very exciting, sometimes life-changing, if they indicate that you have family connections, or ethnic origins, you weren't aware of. But it's only half the story. Now you need to verify the results by cross-referencing them with information you have already collected about your family.

The first part of your test report is about your ethnicity. The company compiles these results by comparing your DNA results with data from reference populations spread across the globe. DNA data is collected from these populations and analysed for markers, or variants, that are more prominent or exclusive to them in specific regions or population groups. We don't suggest using this as the basis to claim membership of a marginalised identity, as this is a sensitive topic for some; it can just be helpful when you are trying to track down branches of your family tree.

By comparing your DNA results with this data, your report will estimate what percentage of your DNA comes from which region. Although the ethnicity report won't identify a specific relative, it could alert you to family in a part of the world you didn't know you were connected with.

As Brad Argent explains, your family research might say where everyone is from, but your ethnicity report could suggest otherwise. 'Let's say I take my DNA test and it comes back and it says, "Oh, look at that. I'm 20 per cent Irish"', says Brad. 'Hang on, hang on. The family story is we're all Scottish, but

I've got this 20 per cent Irish; where is that coming from? You might have been ignoring all those hints for Ireland that popped up in your family tree [on Ancestry], because you're convinced you don't have any Irish ancestry. And then suddenly you get an ethnicity result that says, well, you get 20 per cent from Ireland, maybe you need to go back and have another look. Those are usually the first things that jump out when you look at your results: my ethnicity results don't match with the stories I've been told. Now, either it's because it's telling you something different to what you know, or it's because it's telling you something additional.'

'There are two key pathways a DNA experience can take – confirmation and transformation. Your DNA will tell you something and confirm, ah, look at that. I've got a Spanish ethnicity because there's always been a story that we're connected to Spain. There it is, it's in my DNA. Or, look at that, I have a community in America. I had no idea I had family in America and yet here it is. How awesome. Your results will either confirm what you know, or transform your understanding of your family's origins.'

The second part of your report will show your cousin matching results. They will be listed with the best match – the match that shares the most DNA with you – at the top, with the others in descending order.

Starting with your best match, compare your family tree with each of your DNA cousin matches, and see where they intersect. Cross-reference those intersection points with facts you've gleaned from your other searches – birth, marriage, death certificates, census records and so on.

Once you are sure the match is a good one, you have a significant decision to make: should I contact them? While many distant family members will want to know they have relatives they didn't realise they had, don't assume everyone will want you to contact them. Some people do a DNA test just because they are curious about their ethnic make-up and have no intention of sharing the results with anyone. You might also have discovered there's a link showing that your contact's family tree is very different from the one they currently believe in.

Your best bet is to use your chosen company's internal message system. If the person you are trying to reach out to is open to being contacted, they will have indicated this when they did their test. Data protection is of the utmost importance in DNA testing.

Privacy is paramount

Doing a DNA test as part of your family history research is different from all of the other document or archival research categories. Whether it's a birth certificate, census, shipping record or any other resource that you are scrutinising, you are researching information that already exists. When it comes to a DNA test, you are creating new evidence that is unique to you and potentially making it available to others. The benefit is considerable in that a DNA match could break through a brick wall you have found in your family tree; however, it also allows others to use your data to discover things about their family tree, as well as yours.

As Brad Argent says, we've all become accustomed to clicking 'accept' when we're online, but when it comes to our DNA we need to stop and think first.

'Regardless of what products you're using, when it comes to your genetic material, read the terms and conditions. Understand what control you have over the data that you're providing. And spend some time thinking about it. It's your data. You have every right to take your DNA test. But first think: Do I own the data? Or do they own the data? Because you're testing yourself but you're also in some way testing your siblings and parents. You're potentially testing your children too because you share DNA with them, particularly close DNA. And it shouldn't stop you from doing it because it's your data and you have a right to do with it as you'd feel comfortable. But just remember that the things you uncover will have an impact for other people. And I think it's a really interesting point to drive home, around family history in general. You might be incredibly excited by the discoveries that you make, and other people might not. Think about it before you sit around the Christmas table and just say, "Hey, I found a half sibling in America. I had no idea". That probably won't come as a shock to one of your parents, but it might come as a bit of a shock to the other. So think about how you share any of the information that you have, and the potential impact on the people involved.'

Each of the five main genealogy websites allow you to control how your data is used and accessed. You can choose from various options, such as keeping your data entirely private; allowing limited access (for instance, allowing just your ethnicity results to be viewed); or you can grant complete access. Once you have chosen your preferred company, do take the time to read through their privacy statements and check out their specific privacy management options, as there are differences across the group.

Here's a quick recap of the big five companies currently doing DNA testing:

AncestryDNA does autosomal testing only and currently has the biggest database for cousin matching. If you're looking for the best chance of matches, this is the test for you. Ancestry doesn't allow you to upload DNA data from other testing sites but does allow you to download your raw DNA data. Visit ancestry.com.au/dna for more details.

23andMe does autosomal as well as mtDNA and Y-DNA testing. Visit 23andme.com for more details.

MyHeritage DNA works from a cheek swab rather than saliva and will provide a report on your ethnicity and potential family matches via your autosomal DNA. It allows upload of DNA data from other sites to compare with their own database. Visit myheritage.com/dna for more details.

Family Tree DNA offers testing in all three areas – autosomal, mtDNA and Y-DNA – for varying costs. Many genealogists recommend this one if you want to understand more about your maternal or paternal lines through DNA. It allows you to upload DNA data from other sites. Visit familytreedna.com for more details.

LivingDNA will give you basic information about your ethnicity, specialising in African, European, British and Irish descent. It has the smallest database of all five but offers all three types of testing. It allows upload of DNA data from other sites. Visit livingdna.com/au for more details.

And remember, if you want to use the cousin match service, you will need to allow your data to be accessed by others on the site that you have chosen. It could very well, as in Charlotte's case, turn out to be life-changing.

CHAPTER 12

Land records, censuses and electoral rolls

***AT A GLANCE**: Here we look at records that help place our ancestors at specific points in time and place. We'll discuss where to go to find them, how to use them as research tools and some tips to glean less obvious information.*

> Buy land, they're not making it any more.
>
> Mark Twain

History shows that many in the developed world have taken up Mark Twain's advice, and done so with gusto. Owning your own home is the quintessential Australian dream, and it began soon after the first colonists arrived here. Governor Phillip started the process of issuing land grants in 1789, in the belief that the land belonged to the Crown and not the Aboriginal clans of the Eora nation. It was the genesis of a system of property ownership that exists to this day.

Because there are voluminous quantities of records of all kinds detailing every type of land or property transaction, if your ancestor owned land or property, you may find a record detailing what they bought, what they paid for it and who they might have sold it to, as well as a map showing where it was, among many other documents. Successfully hunting down those records will mean you get access to a level of detail about your ancestor's life that most other records will not give you.

And you never know what you might unearth, as our expert, Carole Riley, found. Carole is a Fellow and past Vice President of the Society of Australian Genealogists. She is also Honorary Editor of their journal *Descent* and author of *Land Research for Family Historians in Australia and New Zealand*, and was doing some research for one of her clients into an ancestor called Langford.

This research became one of Carole's favourite stories, as she explains: 'William Langford and his brother Thomas were transported to Sydney in 1821 for stealing from a boat on the Thames in London. He was recorded as a boat builder in the colony, and worked for the colonial government as such until his time was served.

'I followed his history – his marriage, children, and buying a property on Clyde Street, Millers Point on the water line. It is marked on maps as 'Langford Boat Builder'. His two surviving sons became boat builders, based in the same property until they both died young in 1880/1881, one of phthisis, and one in an accident in a timber yard, and their widows sold it. Their sons mostly became boat builders as well. They were famous for their racing yachts. Clyde Street is no longer there, after The Rocks was totally reconfigured in the early 1900s, but there are photos of the street and the houses taken before they were all knocked down.'

But it was what came next that was a revelation.

Carole's client was contacted by a cousin who had heard about an archaeological dig taking place on Langford's Millers Point land and suggested they should visit the site.

Carole takes up the story: 'I knew where the land was and had all the old system deeds involved, including a bit of extra land reclaimed below the water line. The archaeological report before the dig said they weren't expecting to find anything significant, but they were wrong.

'The team made a dramatic discovery: the well preserved remains of a boat, possibly the oldest locally built boat found in Australia. It was a thrill to see it, still being worked on by marine archaeologists, and the sandstone remains of the building they lived and worked in.

'This story has everything – convicts, early colonial Sydney, old maps, land used as a business as well as a home, and a historic discovery. And I learnt so much about boats and boat-building!'

Now the chances of finding something as dramatic as this in your ancestor's records are remote. But you are likely to find a map showing where your ancestor's property was, for instance. By comparing that map with the online version from Google Maps of today, you could be staring at the plot, or even the building, where your ancestor lived. Discovering a map can lead you to records that might tell you things such as: the type of house they lived in, its location and how many bedrooms it had; if it's a rural property such as a farm, you can find out what they grew and what livestock they owned. Maps also show information about the neighbours. Gathered together, this kind of detail will give you an insight into your family's social and economic standing at the time, and bring their lives into sharper focus.

That's the upside. Now all you need to do is navigate your way through the twists and turns of the world of land records to find the right one! But, and there's a big *but*, searching for land records can be quite tricky. We strongly recommend you immerse yourselves in all the other types of records first before tackling land records. Our expert guide, Carole Riley, agrees: 'It's not like buying birth, death and marriage certificates and just building a tree. Land records can fill out somebody's story, but the land departments were not set up for this; they are a government bureaucracy to keep track of the ownership and transfer of land and property. Their main customers are conveyancers, not family historians. So you already have a tree, you know who all the children are, who the parents are, the grandparents, where they came from, where they lived. Land records can tell you how they lived. So did they own a house? Did they have multiple mortgages? Were they moving from place to place? Did the land form part of their business? Were they farmers, graziers, boatbuilders? Land can be part of their lives in that way, not just the house that they lived in, but what they did for a living. Many people find searching land records very difficult and just give up. Even people who have been to one of my talks, sometimes more than once, would then say to me, "Oh look, it's too hard. Can you do it for me?" But it's worth it. It's definitely worth it.'

Asking someone to do some of the heavy lifting for you is a perfectly legitimate way forward. If you're struggling, seek support from an expert; in fact, we recommend that you do just that. State libraries and archives have people who can help you. The state archives' and land departments' websites in each state have comprehensive guides to searching land records. It's well worth devoting some time to reading them as they are focused on their individual record-keeping conventions.

> **TOP TIP** Use the opportunity to visit the state archives in person, if you can. All of the archivists we have talked with say 'ask us for help, it's part of our job to help people'. They will be able to steer you in the right direction regarding the records they hold, and may also know how to search the lands department website for records available online that the archives don't hold. But they won't do the actual search for your ancestor's records; that's down to you.

But even if you are asking someone else for help, having a basic understanding of how land records work will save you a lot of time, and energy. Which is where we come in. This chapter will take you through some of the things you will encounter, and where you might find them.

Some terms to start you off

The problem with searching for land and property records is there are many systems and numbering conventions, and, of course, there are differences from state to state, not to mention between some of the terms used.

We're sure you will have heard of terms like Torrens Title, parish and squatting, but you will also discover phrases and words like Old System deeds, hundreds, roods and perches. You can be forgiven if you thought the latter two were related to a fishing trip instead of being measurements of land – 1 acre equals 4 roods, and 1 rood equals 40 perches.

To get you started, we have compiled a list opposite of the most commonly used terms for easy reference.

COMMON TERMS YOU'LL COME ACROSS

Alienation In property law this is the process where an owner of property sells the title of their property to a buyer. In this context it was the Crown that was alienated by granting the land to a new owner or tenant.

Auriferous land Land that contains gold.

Common Law contracts or Old System title deeds The practice, imported from England, of drawing up contracts or deeds for each transaction concerned with the buying and selling of land and property.

Cadastral maps A register of graphical representations of the boundaries of properties and land, including other details like ownership and type of use.

County A division of land for administrative purposes. Counties were sub-divided into parishes or hundreds.

Parish A sub-division of a county.

Hundreds Rural land in South Australia was divided into hundreds, around 100 square miles.

Muster The gathering together of people in a specific area to allow authorities to gather information about them and their land.

Acre A land measurement – about 4050 square metres.

Roods A land measurement – 1 acre equals 4 roods.

Perches A land measurement – 1 rood equals 40 perches.

Torrens Title The system of registering land ownership. All transactions in one place, instead of tracing individual deeds. Ownership guaranteed by the government.

What's the first step?

We have already mentioned how important it is to be armed with as much confirmed information about your family as you can find before launching into your research. That's particularly relevant when searching land records. Where your ancestors' records are being held will determine your approach to searching for them, as each state has their own filing system. It's worth remembering what Carole Riley said earlier: these systems were set up to be used by conveyancers, not family historians – some institutions are more accessible than others.

In the world of land records, there are two key institutions in each state – the Land Registry (aka Lands Department and Department of Lands) and the state archives. Fortunately, although there are differences from state to state, the two organisations follow similar processes. You will come across headings such as Colonial Secretary records, Name Indexes, Purchasers and Vendors Indexes, and Torrens Title and Old System deeds, among many others.

Because ease of access to land registry records varies from state to state, we suggest you start by doing an online search in your state archive. They hold many records and indexes that have been digitised, with more and more becoming available all the time. They also have a number of very helpful guides explaining how to use their systems.

Whether you're searching recent deeds or very early grants, the common thread is land. So at the very least you should try and ascertain what state and town your ancestor lived in and, ideally, when they might have lived there – it will give you a head start when you start searching the records.

And as Carole says: 'Begin with your family; get what you can from them. The stories, identify the photos, you know, who's this guy with grandma sort of thing? I didn't get those things from my grandparents because I wasn't interested when they were alive. Fortunately, I had a cousin who was, and my sister heard some stories. I've now got all of my grandmother's photo albums. There are so many photos of holidays and all that sort of thing. It's good to jump onto a computer and start researching the tree but talk to them as soon as you can. Talk to your parents, your grandparents. The stories about the family farm, the house that Great-Granddad owned or, perhaps, the local business they ran, may well be true. Even if some of the information is a little inaccurate, it will give you a possible location to kick off your search.'

Hopefully by the time you get around to searching land records, you will already have interrogated archives like newspapers, wills and BDMs and discovered numerous records about your ancestor's life – as per our previous chapters. But if you're still not convinced about the veracity of the address you have found, there are some other options specifically relating to address details that could be very helpful.

TOP TIP Knowing where your ancestor lived is so important. The go-to resources for finding your ancestor's property or land and their associated land records, including deeds, is searching the indexes by name and knowing at least their county, parish or town, or by scouring a local parish map. Either way, if you don't have a fair idea of where they lived, it's going to be the proverbial needle in a haystack search – if you can locate the right haystack first, that is!

Musters, censuses, electoral rolls and directories

Musters and censuses might be useful if your Australian ancestors go back to the early days of the colonies, but you will need to have a bit of luck on your side. Why? Because, sadly, only some of the musters exist today; some have been lost, while others in New South Wales were destroyed by fire. But at least some of them have survived.

An easy way of finding out if a muster (or census) exists is via State Library Victoria. They have a handy research guide section with a list detailing the ones that have survived. They are arranged on a state-by-state basis. You can find the guides at guides.slv.vic.gov.au/earlycensus.

When it comes to census records it's a similar story, but with one extra layer. You can find records of the statistics the authorities extracted from the original census forms; things like how many rooms in a particular dwelling, how many people lived there, where they were from, and so on, but that detail won't include the names of anyone who lived at the address. That's because, very disappointingly for family historians, many census forms with those householder returns were deliberately destroyed for privacy reasons. But some have survived. Graham Jaunay's very helpful website lists those that have, and where you can locate them. Visit jaunay.com/auscensus.html for more details.

While you might struggle to find your ancestor's address in the musters and census records, you may have a better outcome when searching the electoral rolls. There were elections in the various colonies as early as the mid-1800s. As Carole Riley explains, 'Electoral rolls are also useful for people who did not own the property they lived in. As are rates records.'

WHAT'S THE DIFFERENCE BETWEEN A MUSTER AND A CENSUS?

Colonial musters were done by gathering people together in one spot so the authorities could gather the information they needed. The early musters were carried out primarily to understand what kind of food was required in an area and for how many people. The first muster was done as early as 1788, with the first colonial census being conducted in New South Wales in 1828.

Census returns were done at the person's place of residence and the information was gathered together to create statistical records of the time.

Initially, the right to vote was based on owning or leasing a property over a certain value, and it was usually only men over the age of 21 who were entitled to vote. In Victoria, New South Wales, South Australia and Tasmania, this included Aboriginal men in colonial state elections. No women's names would appear on the colonial election rolls for decades. Women finally won the right to vote in the South Australia colony in 1894; this included Aboriginal women. Other colonies followed suit, ending with Victoria in 1908. However, in Queensland (1885) and Western Australia (1893), laws were passed that denied Aboriginal and Torres Strait Islander people the vote.

In 1901, the six colonies – New South Wales, South Australia, Western Australia, Victoria, Queensland and Tasmania – formed the Commonwealth of Australia. The first federal election was in the same year, but only men were eligible to vote.

Women voted in the second federal election in 1903, having been granted the right to vote – as well as stand for parliament – in 1902. Aboriginal and Torres Strait Islander people didn't get the right to vote in federal elections until 1962.

The National Library of Australia (NLA) has a complete set of Commonwealth electoral rolls, accessible on microfiche up to 2008, and paper rolls to 2009. From 1990 onwards you can search by name in each state; for dates prior to that you will need to know the electorate, subdivision and polling place. If you don't have this information already you can find it by consulting the Australian Electoral Commission (AEC). Early colonial electoral rolls can be found in the NLA collection as well as those in state libraries. The commercial genealogy sites like Ancestry and Findmypast also have some electoral rolls.

Another good source of address information, including if your ancestor was renting a property, can be found in various directories like post office, trade and commercial directories as well as phone books, among a number of other publications including almanacs. Perhaps the best-known publisher of all sorts of directories is Sands. The NLA, state libraries and genealogy sites have copies of the various directories where you can find information about properties, residents, businesses and streets. If you do find what you are looking for in one edition, it's well worth tracking that property through the subsequent editions. Information might change; perhaps the block has been subdivided or maybe your ancestor disappears from an address, meaning he or she could have moved away from the area altogether.

Now that you have a name and location, you can start by finding the parish map or the title deed.

Maps

Finding the parish map that relates to the address or location you have is a popular jump-off point. You will find a surprising amount of information on a map. Things such as: the legal description – that is, whether it's a section, allotment or portion; it will show boundaries and other features like roads and rivers; and references to titles, conditional purchases and primary application numbers that you can use to find other records. More on all of these terms and phrases on page 221.

Finding the parish map indicating your ancestor's property or land is one of the simpler pursuits in the world of land records. You can search the interactive maps of the Land Department in your state, online. As always, though, the more accurate your address information is, the easier the search becomes. Once you have found one of the parish maps, you can have fun by comparing it to the ones on Google maps. If there are distinctive features like rivers or winding roads you should be able to find a match. But, as Carole Riley points out, it could be the opposite way around: 'a client can point to the farm house on a Google map and I find it on a parish map by using the roads and rivers'.

However you are searching, you might find your ancestor's house still exists. Just like staring at a photo of your ancestor, or reading their diary, finding where they lived evokes similar strong emotions.

You might also find someone else's name on the piece of land that you thought belonged to your ancestor. That's because it's an older version of the map and the land bears the original title holder's name – that could be the first person to get the grant from the governor. If this happens to you, search other versions of the map. Your ancestor might have bought the land

LAND DIVISION TERMS YOU NEED TO KNOW

You will come across a range of different terms to describe land or property on a parish map. These terms are important not only because they are used on parish maps but they are also used to identify the land or property on title deeds and other land records, not a property's address. Each state is divided into counties, parishes and portions – except in SA, where parishes are known as hundreds (roughly 100 square miles). As Carole Riley points out, 'Surveyed government towns started as sections and allotments, but surrounding rural land was usually subdivided to add to the town, and these will be found called deposited plans, sections and lots. Even today, the title for the house you live in probably has a lot number rather than a street number.'

from the first colonial owner but the parish map hadn't been updated yet. But in New South Wales, the name on the map is always the *first* titleholder, who acquired the land from the Crown. It might also be that the map you have found shows a bank as the owner, because your ancestor may have had a mortgage when the title was first issued. We didn't say land records were easy!

And, as our expert Carole Riley did with her own early family research, check the adjacent parish (and county) maps, as your ancestor might have bought the land 'next door', which is on a different map. '[I had found my ancestor's block of land] – it's a little narrow 40-acre block of land with his name on it. I know what farmland is like in New South Wales – he couldn't have raised a family on that. So where the land was, there's a road because every block had to have access to a road. So I looked at the map for the adjacent parish and sure enough, on the other side of the road directly opposite is another block with his name on it. I was incredibly lucky with this and I wouldn't recommend it as a strategy. Name indexes are much safer. You might know the name of the farm and roughly where it is, but it will be made up of multiple portions – each 40-acre portion will be a separate paddock. Name indexes will point you to all of them.'

Finding your ancestor's land or property on the map is only one step. You need to find the title deeds to go with it to fully understand the background.

Finding the title deeds

Depending on the date range you are searching, you will find three broad categories about deeds: the Old System, Torrens Title, and conversion files, which hold the evidence of the process of converting Old System to Torrens Title, proving the applicant is legally the owner of the land by producing the chain of deeds. In rare cases the original grant from the governor will be in the file. We take you through the basics of each system below.

The Old System (Common Law Title Deeds)

The earliest land records were written requests for land, known as memorials. If approved, an actual grant was drawn up and given to the landholder, and a copy held by the Registrar

General, later the Lands Department. The Colonial Secretary kept registers of these grants. These were often small pockets of land for convicts – whose sentence had been completed – to grow food for themselves and the colony. These records still exist and can be found in the Colonial Secretary category in the NSW State Archives on the Museums of History NSW website. Similarly, check the other states' archives for their early colonial secretary records too.

Along with the boundaries of your ancestor's portion or allotment, the map of your ancestor's land will contain a lot of information. Unfortunately, most of it will look like it's written in a secret code, but the acronyms and numbers are the clues you need to find the records.

Along with finding another block of her family's land, Carole discovered a 'CP number' on the map, meaning the land was part of a government scheme called conditional purchase, Carole explains: 'A conditional purchase was a way of getting small farmers onto the land to grow food because a lot of the land was taken up by graziers – squatters who got 2000 acres and they weren't growing food, wheat and vegetables and things like that. So they tried to break up some of this land by acquiring some of it and carving it up into 40-acre blocks and offering conditional purchases. So you paid a deposit – it was one pound an acre and you had to live on the land. You had to improve it, fence it and clear it and you were inspected after three years.'

Conditional purchases were one of a number of ways land changed ownership in the early colonial days. The government of the time had set up administrative systems for the control of land that had been annexed in the monarch's name – which is why it became known as Crown Land.

SOME RECORDS YOU MIGHT FIND

Conditional purchases or conditional leases Land was granted on the proviso that it would be improved; for example, built on, fenced, and/or crops grown.

Pastoral leases Approval for land to be used for livestock grazing.

Soldier settlements A scheme for returned soldiers to acquire land to farm. But the land wasn't always good farming land and the ex-soldier may not have known anything about farming. Many families walked off the land when they couldn't make a living and pay off the government.

Special leases Perhaps to be used to build something like a wharf or a boat shed.

Torrens Title

A new land registration system came into being in the mid-1800s, with the passing into law of the Real Property Act – we know this system as Torrens Title. It was devised by Sir Robert Torrens, a South Australian statesman. As the Collector of Customs in Adelaide in 1840, he advocated for the system of recording in one document the ownership and dealings of ships. He became convinced the system could be adapted for land records. His election to the South Australia parliament in 1857 presented an opportunity to table his Land Administration Bill. It faced minimal opposition and resulted in the *Real Property Act 1858*.

The key feature of the act was the creation of a Certificate of Title where all interests in a property, including transfers, mortgages, leases and any other dealings are recorded in a single document. Once registered by the appropriate State land authority, the validity of the Certificate of Title was guaranteed by the State.

It was adopted by different states at different times, as the table opposite shows.

As Carole Riley explains, Torrens Title transformed land records. 'A Torrens Title was, in the early days, two sides of a piece of paper and it will have a description of the land and a plan and when it was registered and then it will have every transaction relating to that piece of land – that's why Torrens Title is important. Your ownership was guaranteed by the government and all the information about it, all the transactions and changes of ownership, were held in one place. Whereas the previous system, the Old System, or Common Law title system that we inherited from England, you had to have the chain of deeds. So you had to have every deed to prove that that land was yours.'

So if you are searching after the Real Property Acts were introduced, you're in luck. The benefit of having every transaction on one deed means Torrens Title records are a boon for landowners and family historians alike. The previous system, the Old System, only noted the details of the 'buyer and seller' of a single transaction. Which means, if you find an early 'old' deed it will tell you who owned or sold a particular property on one date. If that property changed hands before or after that date you would have to start another search because Old System deeds don't mention details about the previous owner. Whereas with a Torrens Title, in most cases you can trace land ownership back to the first grant, as every transaction to do with that property will be detailed within that one document. If the piece of paper is filled with transactions, or the land changes, for example, it's split into two, then a new title will be issued, and each will refer to the other so you can go backwards and forwards.

TORRENS TITLE DATES FOR EACH STATE

SA	1858	NSW	1863
QLD	1862	ACT	1863
VIC	1862	WA	1876
TAS	1862		

Conversion of Old System to Torrens Title

After the introduction of Torrens Title, each state began to convert Old System land records into Torrens system titles. Unfortunately, the conversion process has different names – in New South Wales it's called a primary application (PA); in Victoria it's a conversion application (CA); while in South Australia it's known as a title application (TA). If you find one of these acronyms on a parish map followed by a number, for example, PA 12345, this shows, in this case, that it's a primary application and the number identifies the sequential application number. It will lead you to the application packet. So search indexes for both Old System and Torrens Title deeds. These indexes will be in the state archives or the lands department.

Before an Old System deed could be converted to Torrens Title, owners had to put in a detailed application and offer evidence of the chain of title proving they were indeed the rightful owners. This could include: previous grants or deeds under the Old System – possibly signed by the governor; death and marriage certificates; wills and probate records; correspondence; anything that proved their right to be the new Torrens Title owner. These packets are a veritable treasure trove of family information. You can find most of these documents in your states' land registry or the state archives in record series called primary application or deposited deeds packets. The latter are so called because these are packets containing the documents that were lodged with the lands registry for safe keeping as part of a chain of title process. In South Australia you need the permission of the current title holder, and in NSW the application form has been separated from the packet, so request both.

As we have shown, because buying and selling property and land requires a chain of title, the authorities will have required any number of documents to prove ownership. It's not unheard of to find a document in land records that has 'gone missing' elsewhere. Whether you manage to do a land record search yourself or engage someone to do it on your behalf, you could discover a wealth of information about your family.

And, as Carole Riley discovered, paying a visit to an ancestor's home or land can pay dividends. Carole had been researching land records to investigate her family's farming heritage, and found where her great-grandfather's land was, so decided to make the trip: 'I wanted to see where it was and what it looked like because you see it on a map and it's just all flat'.

While she was there she bumped into the current owner by the farm gate. 'I was standing in the grass talking to the owner about our families' histories, when he said "wait here" and he drove off over the hill. He came back with a photograph of

John Eason, my great-grandfather, standing on the verandah of his house at "Fernside" with his dog at his side. It is the only photo of him we have ever seen.'

All of which is a great reminder to talk to whomever you can – your family, archivists and family history societies. You never know what could turn up.

CHAPTER 13

Oral, film and photographic archives

***AT A GLANCE**: These records can often be overlooked but are well worth the investment of time. Institutions including state libraries and archives, the National Film and Sound Archive and local libraries and councils hold a wealth of photographic images, audio and visual recordings that can bring our ancestors to life. Here we offer a few examples of what you may find.*

> Oral tradition is very strong within Aboriginal communities. I trust those stories 90 per cent of the time.
>
> SLNSW librarian Melissa Jackson, Bundjalung woman

By now, you will have amassed all manner of facts about your ancestors: where and when they were born; if they married; where they lived; what they gave to whom in their will. Oral, film and photographic archives can help complete a picture of their lives, by colouring in the blank spaces between the facts and give their lives context.

Your ancestors may have lived through one, or more, significant historic event, such as a gold rush, one or both world

DID YOU KNOW? The earliest known surviving photograph in Australia was taken between late 1844 and early 1845. The daguerreotype is part of the State Library of NSW's collection and is a portrait of Dr William Bland, an ex-convict and surgeon who, after being pardoned in 1815, became the first doctor to establish a private practice in the colony.

wars, and the Great Depression. Can you imagine the impact any one of those would have had on their day-to-day lives? What if their homes were inundated by floods, or perhaps their community was savaged by a ferocious bushfire? What kind of community did they live in, what celebrations brought them together? What topics were being talked about in the newspapers, pubs and cafes? By unearthing the answers to some or all of these questions you will create a holistic view of your ancestor's life.

You can get an insight into your ancestor's world by searching the archives for photographs, oral histories, audio and, more recently, film and video recordings. We suggest a number of options below.

Photographs

These still images are so evocative, whether they're of people, buildings or landscapes. You're immediately taken back to another time. So often the subject of the picture is looking straight at the camera; it's as if they are staring directly at you. Shaun was only two when his father passed away; he recalls the moment he saw his photograph for the first time: 'I felt an eerie and instant connection with this man who I'd never got to know. It kickstarted my quest to find out who he was'.

There are also many clues hidden in plain sight: the clothes people are wearing; the location they are in; the street and shop names; maybe there are horse-drawn carriages or cars in the picture; or perhaps key buildings are being constructed. Each element can tell you something more about what was happening at the time – these images are a moment frozen in time, and even if they're not of your ancestors, they will still give you a glimpse of life as it was.

Family historians can find a substantial cache of these images across a number of state and private institutions. Here are some of the key repositories.

If you have been researching newspaper articles that might be about your ancestor and your search has taken you to Trove, you'll know how valuable it is. But for any family historian searching from the early 19th century onwards, their photographic archive is equally beneficial. Along with the photographs, their collection also holds prints, drawings, cartoons, paintings, architectural plans, printed ephemera and maps.

Say, for instance, that your ancestor was living around the time of the Great Depression; select the 'Images, Maps and Artefacts' category from the drop-down menu on the Trove search box, and then type 'Great Depression Australia' and you will be offered numerous pictures from across Australia.

But the next step is where it gets even better. If there's a particular image that attracts your attention, select the 'Newspapers and Gazettes' tab, add the photograph's date to the wording of your original search and press search again. Trove will show you a range of newspaper articles to go with the photo you've found. Along with the pictures, you will have the journalist's commentary on that era.

It's likely that when you do an image search on Trove, the results will be a mix of thumbnail images and other entries where the thumbnail is a blank box. This means that image is not online, usually because it isn't part of the National Library of Australia (NLA) collection, but it is available in another archive. If you click on the image it will give you more detail about where you can access it.

If the image is displayed in the thumbnail, you may be able to purchase a copy of your own. Click on the picture and select the 'Buy' button. You will see a link that will direct you to the NLA's website or, if the NLA doesn't hold the image, the link will take you to the archive that does.

You will also find a rich source of images in each state library. In fact, many of the blank screen thumbnails in Trove will be those held at the various state libraries. But check your own state library's website anyway just in case one of their images has slipped the net. And don't forget to look in your city or local library too, especially if you have tracked your ancestor down to a specific city or town. These collections might yield surprising results. Many of them have their own smaller archives as well as links to other local collections dedicated to that area. Along with searching the various local libraries, you will find other photographs and ephemera in the city councils' own archives.

Back to Trove for a moment: it also has a category called Diaries, Letters and Archives. This is the place to find things such as letters, diaries and handwritten notes. There are also unpublished draft manuscripts, press clippings and ephemeral items like official invitations, programs and even menus. You will also discover published government reports and reviews on a variety of subjects. Hours – sometimes days – of reading await you!

TOP TIP Some institutions, such as state libraries, allow you to download digitised out-of-copyright images for free. These are usually in either a low-resolution or high-resolution format. Just be sure to check the relevant usage policy to understand how you can use them.

And the list goes on! Your individual state's archives also have huge collections of images. Quite often, these will be pictures taken by professional photographers working for the various state departments. You will find their work under headings like school reports, public works, maritime support, railways and land records. Do a general search on your state archives' websites to discover how they have named their categories – category descriptions differ from state to state.

Think also about how your ancestor interacted with the government and when a photograph of them may have been taken. Gaol records, for instance, are often accompanied by photographs from the mid- to late 1800s and can sometimes be the only photographic record of a person, as was the case with one of Cassie's ancestors in the late 1800s.

The National Archives of Australia (NAA) is another institution that operates on a nationwide scale, like Trove. It also has both photographic images and contextual material that complement each other and add a depth of understanding to any search. By doing your search in the Basic Search tab in the Record Search area on their website, you will find a list of everything the NAA archive has for the wording you type in. This could be articles, photographs and even audiovisual material (more about that in a moment). Some of the items will be digitised but many might not, so you will need to note the item number and request it. There are two options: you can view the item in one of the NAA's research centres in each capital city, or you can buy a digital copy of your own, for a fee.

If your search turns up an ancestor who was in the Australian Defence Force, there is a wealth of photographic material to be found in the Australian War Memorial's (AWM) collection – 312 057 photographs and counting. You would have to be very lucky to find a photo of your ancestor but you will be able to get images that showcase military life at home and abroad. Their collection dates back to the Crimean War and includes every war or conflict that Australian soldiers served in. Select the 'Collections' tab on the AWM homepage and then 'Photograph' from the icons displayed lower down on the page. You can then filter your search by selecting the war, unit or place from the list on the left of the page. The results will show what is available. For more detail on searching the AWM, please refer to chapter 10 on military records.

The national museums and those in your state's capitals have collections that are worth investigating too. You can also add universities to that list; some are home to well-known collections like the Macleay Collection held by Sydney University. And don't forget your local family history society too; even if they don't have an archive of their own, they are sure to know where there are ones you can try.

Subscription sites such as Ancestry and Findmypast have photographic archives searchable online as well. These are generally collections of images of ancestors that people have uploaded to their family tree and are searchable if public access is allowed, and collections from institutions that have been digitised by the site. With the former, as always, you'll want to try and do your own research to ensure that the image that someone says is of an ancestor actually is, but it is exciting if you can put a face to an ancestor's name! We had experience of this when someone sent us a photograph of Cassie's paternal grandfather before he migrated to Australia in 1922. The image was one that Cassie's father had never seen.

Ancestry is a good example of the latter types of images – ones that they have acquired permission to digitise. Although their current collection is still relatively small – currently about 7000 images – it can contain things that you may not expect to find. The experience of Ancestry's very own Brad Argent is a great example. Out of curiosity one day, Brad started exploring the 'Sydney Harbour Bridge Construction, 1922–1933' collection of photographs on Ancestry. Brad takes up the story: 'I love the photographs because they're not full of people and they're not names and dates and places. It's a single event. And you get a sense of what it was like in this part of Australia at this period in history. And now I have a personal connection to them – I found a photograph of my grandmother within this collection. The only photograph that exists of her as a child!' Brad explains how he knew it was his grandmother: 'We were walking across the Sydney Harbour Bridge for its 75th anniversary and my grandmother mentioned being at the opening with her classmates. She would have been 13 at the time and I recall being somewhat sceptical as the event was no place for a young girl (particularly one with my grandmother's diminutive stature). When I came upon that photograph I realised that she had the date wrong – a bit of work on Trove told me school groups attended in the lead-up to the opening. When I showed her the photograph the memories resurfaced.'

Although in Brad's own words, finding the image was a 'massive fluke', it just goes to show that it's worth looking through collections if you have the time. 'I don't think I'll ever replicate that sort of find. But I've had it once and I wouldn't have had it if I didn't just browse through the collection.'

Flickr is another site you may have come across. It's a good source for historical images as many cultural institutions upload collections there. You can follow, tag and comment on images if you sign up for a free account. Go to flickr.com for more information.

All in all, your searches for photographic images and ephemera will produce a rich collection of snapshots and articles that will give you a rounded and fascinating picture of what your ancestor's life looked and felt like.

Oral and audiovisual history

We have alluded to oral history in previous chapters, when we suggested that you gather information from the oldest members of your family by interviewing them. Oral histories are a time capsule containing the intimate details of your family's life. We have adapted an old African proverb that so accurately articulates the knowledge held by our ancestors: 'Every old [person] that dies is a library that burns'. First Nations peoples have passed knowledge from generation to generation through the spoken word for thousands of years; it's an integral part of their culture. In more recent times, a number of institutions, as well as members of the public, have begun to conduct interviews across a range of topics and cultures to include in their collections. These can be written accounts of the interview, sound recordings or audiovisual recordings. These same organisations are home to a broad collection of other oral and audiovisual material – broadcast programs, actuality recordings, speeches and public events.

Part of librarian Melissa Jackson's role at SLNSW is to interview Indigenous communities and record family histories. A big part of doing so involves gaining the trust of community, Melissa says. 'We're yet to get that leverage in. I'm Bundjalung, and Sydney born and bred. My boss is Palawa; he's from Tasmania. My other colleague is Bundjalung. But it's about getting that leverage into community for them to trust us enough. It's got to do with, you know, do you trust a government department regardless of who is conducting the interview? I think that will occur once we get to that tipping point, but it's because your personal information, your family history, your community history is very important. It's meaningful to you and your people, but because it was written down in documents and shared amongst government, you know, all of that type of stuff when the Protection Board was around, you had no control over it. Your knowledge became public knowledge. So people are rightly wanting to keep their cultural identities, [and their] cultural histories. We just have to build up the trust.'

When searching for oral and audio histories, Trove's Music, Audio and Video category is a great place to start. This is where you'll find recordings of interviews, lectures, and music. Some of the catalogue items will be the original recordings from the date range you are searching, while others might be documentary productions or talks about the events of that time. The latter group may contain excerpts from the original recordings as part of their storyline. Many of these programs have been put together by the ABC's Radio National production teams and, later, those from ABC Television. Other government-funded projects and commercial companies also produced material on different subjects. The item you come across will identify who was responsible for it and whether there are any copyright restraints.

Some of these recordings are available online, but many are not, so you have three choices: visit the archive where the item is stored; request and pay a fee for your own copy; or check if you can use the interlibrary scheme where you can have the item sent to your local library (check with them to see if this service is available and at what cost).

The NAA also has a significant catalogue in this category. The collection lists records for the ABC and the Department of Information's Film Division, as well as material produced by a range of Commonwealth agencies involved in national defence, commissions of inquiry, celebrations and commemorative events. There are also personal records of ministers, including past prime ministers, governors-general and judges.

Items in this category are stored on a range of media; for example, film, tape, video and CD. You might be lucky and find you can listen to or view what you have found, but many aren't available online. You will need to note the item number you have found and access it in one of the NAA's reading rooms located in each capital city. If you are unable to get to a reading room, you can buy a digital copy of your own, for a fee.

The AWM has an extensive library of film and sound recordings documenting the lives of Australian Defence Force personnel while in uniform. These recordings have been produced by individuals and companies, including the ABC, SBS, the Department of Veterans Affairs and films made by the AWM itself, as well as commercial organisations and individuals who have recorded interviews for posterity.

Your search for both Sound and Film records might surprise you; those two groups contain nearly 12 000 items. There is even footage dating back to the Boer War (1899–1902).

The search terms are similar to the photograph search: select the 'Collections' tab on the AWM homepage and then

'Film' or 'Sound' from the icons displayed lower down on the page. You can then filter your search by selecting the war, unit or place from the list on the left of the page.

If you are searching in the 'Film' category, there is an option to filter for 'A Last Post Film'. These films are recordings of the AWM commemoration ceremonies that are performed each day. The focus of each ceremony is the story behind one of the names on the Roll of Honour – Australians who have died at war or on other operations. There is a transcript of the speech and video of the event but there isn't footage of the person or their unit. So unless you are looking for a specific name, these films are of less use for family research than others in this category.

The National Film and Sound Archives (NFSA) started collecting material in 1984 and has amassed more than 4 million works, and it's growing all the time. Their collection includes videos, audio tapes, records, compact discs, phonograph cylinders and wire recordings, as well as feature films, TV series, radio shows, even video games, although the last category might not yield too much by way of family history!

As you are looking for contextual material to better understand your ancestor's life, you should search through the NFSA's curated list. You will find the list by selecting 'Collection' on the NFSA homepage, then 'Explore' from the Curated Collections option. You can search for numerous

TOP TIP When you're searching the NFSA website, add the word 'newsreel' to your search wording or look for newsreels in the results list. That way you get the pictures and an explanation about the content.

topics. You should find a number of online recordings that you can watch at home.

If you prefer to be more specific with your search, you will need to click on 'More' on the NFSA homepage, then select 'Search the Collection', which will offer you a search box with two search options: simple or advanced. The latter allows you to filter where you are searching, for example, film, radio, sound and so on. There is a comprehensive guide called 'Using the Collection'. You can find it by that name when you select 'Collection' on the NFSA homepage.

There are oral accounts and audiovisual records to be found in state and city archives and libraries and, as always, check in with your local family history society. You will not be the first person searching for material.

*

History, whether it's world history, social history or family history, is endlessly fascinating to us. It's also the bedrock of everyone's individual story.

A family historian's quest is a continuing journey. For Cassie, it's finding out more about her Danish ancestry on her father's side. For Shaun, it's taking the next steps to discover more about his father's side. The driving force behind this book is to share our love for history with you and encourage you to research your family's story, build your own tree, and connect with your past. You might find 'lost' photographs and documents, or perhaps identify a branch of the family you never knew you had, or maybe you'll unearth something uncomfortable – whatever it is, it's important. It's the story of you.

Things our experts wish they'd known when starting out

Our experts for this book gave such valuable advice and insights into the world of family history. Here are some things they'd wished someone had said to them when they were getting started:

> Record all the places you looked (whether you were successful or not) – that saves returning to look in the same place again later. Write down everything you find (even if you don't know what it all means) and exactly where you found it, to save having to go back for that extra information later. Your description of where you found it explains your conclusions and adds to the credibility of your research – and also allows someone else to find the same record.
>
> *Kerry Farmer, genealogist*

> One thing that I think is really important for beginners is to know how to budget when you're doing your family history. It doesn't have to be an expensive hobby. One of the mistakes I made early on was buying certified birth, marriage and death certificates, not knowing that in New South Wales, you can get transcriptions of those certificates at a lower price for family history. And you

don't necessarily have to pay for subscriptions to all the family history sites. Most libraries have subscriptions to Ancestry, Findmypast and MyHeritage that library members can access in the library or at home.

Danielle Lautrec, author and genealogist

Ask the very basic questions and build a solid foundation for the research you're doing. Whether that's asking a librarian, an archivist or someone at your local family history society, don't assume that you're the first one to ask, because it's more likely than not that 100 other people have asked that question. Don't reinvent the wheel if you don't need to.

Peter Edwards, librarian, SLWA

Firstly I wish someone had told me this was going to be a lifelong obsession! When you first start out you don't realise how addictive it can actually become. But in all seriousness, I think it probably does get back to the fact that we spend a lot of time collecting documentary evidence about our family in all different areas, not just births, deaths and marriages, but shipping arrivals and probate records and land records and whatever else it might be. But always we have to remember that we're dealing with human beings and they had bad days when they're recording information. They gave false information if it suited their purpose. We need the documents but we always have to verify and check everything we find. And I think over the years, I've done a reasonably good job in what I've done. But there have certainly been mistakes I've made that when I look back now I think, 'Why didn't I see that? Why didn't I know that?' And that comes with experience.

Heather Garnsey, genealogist and
Fellow of the Society of Australian Genealogists

Really, really think about how to structure your electronic files. Because I am spending a lot of time at the moment going back and rearranging my electronic files and realising that I have changed the way I've labelled them so many times over the years. Life would be much easier if I had actually just come up with an easy methodology at the start. I think I just didn't realise how much I was going to generate when I started. Like I thought, oh, I'll get a few certificates, you know, maybe a few shipping records. And now I've got thousands of documents. I wish someone had sat me down and said, 'Look, don't leap into this, actually map out how you want to store all this stuff'. (See chapter 3 for advice on organising your files.)

Vanessa Cassin, Education Manager,
Society of Australian Genealogists

> Talk to your family. Ask questions. And when you do that, write down what they say. Years later, when you're doing some research, you'll have a moment when you think 'such and such told me that', but they've sadly passed away and you can't go back and ask them again. But if you've written everything down that they told you, it's like a little resource in itself. And you'll be able to go back and reflect on what they said, and it will help join all the dots.
>
> *Petrina Prowse, Capel District Cemeteries Project*

And from us? Ask questions and record all those family stories that you're told. Then join a family history society. Networking with other family historians will give you a wealth of information as to how they started. They'll also be able to advise you on overcoming any brick walls.

Further resources

Below we've listed references we've mentioned in each chapter so you can see them easily. We've added in some extras that are good for further, more extensive research in Australia and beyond.

General resources

These resources apply throughout the book but are particularly relevant in chapters 1 and 2.

Websites

Ancestry, ancestry.com.au. Ancestry is arguably the best known of the subscription-based genealogy websites. The site offers a 14-day free trial, after which you can swap to a paid subscription. Many libraries offer free access to Ancestry on site.

Australasian Federation of Family History Organisations (AFFHO), affho.org. AFFHO is an umbrella organisation for family history organisations in Australia and New Zealand. You can find contact details for your local society in their membership section.

Australian Joint Copying Project, nla.gov.au/using-library/research-tools-and-resources/australian-joint-copying-project. A collection of historical material relating to Australia, New Zealand and the Pacific dating from 1560–1984.

Australian Institute of Aboriginal and Torres Strait Islander Studies, aiatsis.gov.au. AIATSIS is a national institution dedicated to Aboriginal and Torres Strait Islander culture and history. Their website has a very useful family history section which contains fact sheets with information on all aspects of research.

Biographical Database of Australia, bda-online.org.au. This database is searchable online. It contains information sourced from a number of records dating back to early explorers, the first European settlers of 1788, and Indigenous people.

CoraWeb, coraweb.com.au. This site has links to genealogy websites arranged in categories. Each link has a short summary of what the website covers.

Cyndi's List, cyndislist.com. This site has a comprehensive list of links to genealogical research sites online. Go to 'Categories', then 'Australia' for Australian links.

Dead Reckoning, slwa.wa.gov.au/dead_reckoning. A guide to family history research in Western Australia, updated by the State Library.

Diary of an Australian Genealogist, diaryofanaustraliangenealogist.com. Written by Shauna Hicks, one of Australia's pre-eminent professional genealogists, this site is full of advice, news and events.

FamilySearch, familysearch.org. A not-for-profit genealogy website operated by the Church of Jesus Christ of Latter Day Saints. It has a large collection of digitised online records that can be accessed for free.

Findmypast, findmypast.com.au. Findmypast is a subscription genealogy website. Although their records are predominantly UK-centric, they also have many Australian records. Findmypast offers a 7-day free trial, and some libraries offer free access on site and from home.

GeniAus, geniaus.blogspot.com. Written by genealogist Jill Ball, and covers topics relevant to Australian family history.

Gould Genealogy & History, gould.com.au. Gould is a long-established Australian company specialising in family history products, including their reference book series called Unlock the Past.

Koori Heritage Trust, kht.org.au. An organisation devoted to First Nations peoples of south-east Australia.

MyHeritage, myheritage.com. MyHeritage is a subscription-based genealogy website and has searchable record sets from across the world. Similar to Ancestry and Findmypast, it too offers a 14-day free trial.

Pandora, pandora.nla.gov.au. Also an initiative from the National Library of Australia and now searchable on Trove, the Pandora Archive is a selective collection of web publications and archived websites relating to Australia and Australians.

Trove, trove.nla.gov.au. A collaboration between the National Library of Australia and hundreds of partner organisations around Australia, Trove allows you to search and explore amazing collections from Australian libraries, universities, museums, galleries and archives. And it's completely free.

Libraries

ACT Heritage Library, library.act.gov.au/find/history.
Libraries Tasmania, libraries.tas.gov.au.
Library and Archives NT, lant.nt.gov.au.
National Library of Australia, nla.gov.au.
State Library of New South Wales, sl.nsw.gov.au.
State Library of Queensland, slq.qld.gov.au.
State Library of South Australia, slsa.sa.gov.au.
State Library of Western Australia, slwa.wa.gov.au.
State Library Victoria, slv.vic.gov.au.

Archives

ArchivesACT, archives.act.gov.au.
Library and Archives NT, lant.nt.gov.au.
Museums of History New South Wales, mhnsw.au.
National Archives of Australia, naa.gov.au.
NSW State Archives Collection, mhnsw.au/collections/state-archives-collection.
Public Record Office Victoria, prov.vic.gov.au/explore-collection/where-start.
Queensland State Archives, archivessearch.qld.gov.au.
State Records Office of Western Australia, archive.sro.wa.gov.au.
Tasmanian Archives, libraries.tas.gov.au/tasmanian-archives.

Books

Hicks, Shauna, *Where do I start? A guide to researching your family in Australia and News Zealand*, 2nd edition, 2018, Unlock the Past.
Lautrec, Danielle, *The good genealogist: how to improve the quality of your family history research*, 2022, Society of Australian Genealogists.
O'Neill, Danny (ed), *Family history for beginners and beyond*, 16th edition, 2020, The Heraldry & Genealogy Society of Canberra Inc.

Facebook

There are numerous Facebook groups related to genealogy. The groups vary in size from a handful of members to many thousands; together they form a large community that are passionate about family history and happy to offer research advice to group members.

Chapter 3: Building a family tree

Websites

Canva, canva.com.
Family Tree Maker, mackiev.com/ftm.
Legacy Family Tree, legacyfamilytree.com.
Reunion, available from gould.com.au.

Books

Smith, Drew, *Organize your genealogy: Strategies and solutions for every researcher*, 2016, Family Tree Books.

Chapter 4: Birth, death and marriage records

Websites

Registries of births, deaths and marriages:
Australian Capital Territory, accesscanberra.act.gov.au.
New South Wales, familyhistory.bdm.nsw.gov.au.
Northern Territory, nt.gov.au/law/bdm.
Queensland, familyhistory.bdm.qld.gov.au.
South Australia, cbs.sa.gov.au/births-deaths-marriages; genealogysa.org.au/resources/online-database-search.
Tasmania, libraries.tas.gov.au.
Victoria, bdm.vic.gov.au.
Western Australia, bdm.justice.wa.gov.au.

Books

Farmer, Kerry, *Handy guide: Births, marriages and deaths in Australia*, 2017, Unlock the Past.

Adoption resources and Forgotten Australians

CLAN (Care Leavers Australasia Network), clan.org.au.
Find and Connect, findandconnect.gov.au.
Kyle, Noelene, *Researching your ancestor's childhood*, 2016, Unlock the Past.
Weinberg, Tamar, *The adoptee's guide to DNA testing: How to use genetic genealogy to discover long-lost family*, 2018, Family Tree Books.

Chapter 5: Wills and probate

Websites

Museums of History New South Wales, mhnsw.au.

Books

Hicks, Shauna, *Handy guide: Australian and New Zealand wills and probate records*, 2021, Unlock The Past.

Chapter 6: Cemetery and church records

Websites

Capel District Cemeteries Project, capeldistrictcemeteriesproject.com.au.
Ryerson, ryersonindex.org. This is an index of death notices appearing in Australian newspapers. You may also find obituaries and funeral notices.

Books

Hicks, Shauna, *Finding ancestors in church records: A brief guide to resources*, 2012, Unlock the Past.
Killion, Martyn and Garnsey, Heather (eds), *Cemeteries in Australia: A register of transcripts*, 1994, Australasian Federation of Family History Organisations.

Chapter 7: Convicts

Websites

British Newspaper Archive, britishnewspaperarchive.co.uk.

Chief Secretary's Office Registered Papers (CSORP), National Archives of Ireland, csorp.nationalarchives.ie.

Colonial Secretary Letters Received, 1826–1896, mhnsw.au/indexes/colonial-secretary/colonial-secretary-letters-received-1826-1896.

Colonial Secretary's Papers, mhnsw.au/archive/subjects/colonial-secretary.

Irish Newspaper Archives, irishnewsarchive.com.

London Lives, londonlives.org.

State Records Office of Western Australia, wa.gov.au/organisation/state-records-office-of-western-australia/convicts.

The Proceedings of the Old Bailey, oldbaileyonline.org.

Books

Baxter, Carol, *Guide to convict transportation lists, Part 1, 1787–1800*, 2015, Unlock the Past.

Baxter, Carol, *Guide to convict transportation lists, Part 2, 1801–1812*, 2015, Unlock the Past.

Flynn, Michael, *The Second Fleet: Britain's grim convict armada of 1790*, 2001, Library of Australian History.

Hall, Barbara. *A desperate set of villains: The Convicts of the* Marquis Cornwallis, *Ireland to Botany Bay*, 1796, 2000, self-published.

Hall, Barbara, *A nimble fingered tribe: The convicts of the* Sugar Cane, *Ireland to Botany Bay, 1793*, 2002, self-published.

Hall, Barbara, *Death or liberty: The convicts of the* Britannia, *Ireland to Botany Bay 1797*, 2006, self-published.

Hall, Barbara, *Of infamous character: The convicts of the* Boddingtons, *Ireland to Botany Bay, 1793*, 2004, self-published.

Hall, Barbara, *The Irish vanguard: The convicts of the* Queen, *Ireland to Botany Bay, 1791*, 2009, Irish Wattle.

Hall, Barbara, *The rebel ship* Minerva: *Ireland to New South Wales, 1800*, 2015, Irish Wattle.

Podcasts

The Ironclad Sisterhood, Society of Genealogists.

Chapter 8: Immigration and shipping records

Websites

FamilyHistoryWA, fhwa.org.au.

Kerry Farmer, kerryfarmer.info.

Libraries Tasmania, libraries.tas.gov.au/family-history/arrivals-immigration-and-departures.

Northern Territory Archives Service, navigator.nt.gov.au.

Public Record Office Victoria, prov.vic.gov.au.

Queensland State Archives, data.qld.gov.au/dataset/assisted-immigration-1848-to-1912.
South Australian Maritime Museum, passengers.history.sa.gov.au.
State Archives NSW, mhnsw.au/archive/subjects/immigration-and-shipping.
State Library of New South Wales, sl.nsw.gov.au/shipping_passengers/getting_started.
State Library Victoria, guides.slv.vic.gov.au/migration/getstarted.
State Records of South Australia, archives.sa.gov.au/finding-information/passenger-lists-1845-1940.

Books

Farmer, Kerry, *Arrivals in Australia from 1788*, 2015, Unlock the Past.
Num, Cora, *Shipping and migration research in the internet*, 2nd edition, 2016, Moruya Heads.

Chapter 9: Newspapers and gazettes

Websites

Trove, trove.nla.gov.au.

Books

Hicks, Shauna, *Discover genealogy treasure in the National Library of Australia*, 2nd edition, 2016, Unlock the Past.

Chapter: 10 Military records

Websites

Archives New Zealand, archives.govt.nz.
Australian War Memorial, awm.gov.au.
Commonwealth War Graves Commission, cwgc.org.
Gallipoli Association, gallipoli-association.org.
Library and Archives Canada, library-archives.canada.ca.
The Great War Forum, greatwarforum.org.
The Imperial War Museum, iwm.org.uk.
The National Archives UK, discovery.nationalarchives.gov.uk.

Books

Smith, Neil, *Australians in peril: Tracing your World War Two Australian military ancestors*, 2017, Unlock the Past.
Smith, Neil, *Military research: Getting the most out of your digger's military records*, 2018, Unlock the Past.
Smith, Neil, *Understanding Australian Military Speak*, 2016, Unlock the Past.
Smith, Neil, *What's in a name: Aliases of the Australian Military Forces 1914–1919*, 1995, Mostly Unsung Military History Research and Publications.

Stanley, Peter, *Bad characters: Sex, crime, mutiny, murder and the Australian imperial force*, 2010, Pier 9.
Stanley, Peter, *Charles Bean: Man, myth, legacy*, 2017, NewSouth Publishing.
Stanley, Peter, *Digger Smith and Australia's Great War: Ordinary name – extraordinary stories*, 2011, Pier 9.

Chapter 11: Who's in your DNA?

Websites

23andMe, 23andme.com/en-int.
Ancestry DNA, ancestry.com.au/dna.
DNA & Genealogy, geniel.au.
Family Tree DNA, familytreedna.com.
GEDmatch, gedmatch.com.
International Society of Genetic Genealogy, isogg.org.
LivingDNA, livingdna.com/au.
MyHeritage DNA, myheritage.com/dna.

Books

Farmer, Kerry, *DNA chromosome mapping*, 2018, Unlock the Past.
Farmer, Kerry, *DNA for genealogists*, 4th edition, 2017, Unlock the Past.

Chapter 12: Land records, censuses and electoral rolls

Websites

Heritage Genealogy (Carole Riley), heritagegenealogy.com.au.
Graham Jaunay, jaunay.com/auscensus.html.
State Library Victoria, guides.slv.vic.gov.au/earlycensus.

Books

Riley, Carole, *Land research for family historians in Australia & New Zealand 2nd edition*, 2023, Unlock the Past.

Chapter 13: Oral, film and photographic archives

Websites

Flickr, flickr.com.
National Film and Sound Archive of Australia, nfsa.gov.au.
Portrait Detective, portraitdetective.com.au.

Podcasts

Portrait Detective, Cassie Gilmartin and Margot Riley. The History Crew and State Library of New South Wales.

Acknowledgements

It takes a team to make a book and there are many people to whom we'd like to extend our grateful thanks.

To our wonderful publisher Harriet McInerney for believing in us. Without your support this book would not have happened.

To the equally stellar editing team, Sophia Oravecz, Jocelyn Hungerford and Gabriella Sterio, wonderfully talented designers Lisa White and Josephine Pajor-Markus, and everyone at UNSW Press who helped us every step of the way.

To our incredibly knowledgeable experts for giving us your time and wisdom: Brad Argent, Jen Baldwin, Carol Baxter, Vanessa Cassin, Alison Dellit, Peter Edwards, Kerry Farmer, Michael Flynn, Heather Garnsey, Maxine Gray, Emily Hanna, Amanda King-Hardie, Melissa Jackson, Danielle Lautrec, Jack Martin, Petrina Prowse, Carole Riley, Professor Peter Stanley and John Warren – this book has benefitted immeasurably from your expertise.

To Vanessa Cassin and Ruth Graham from the Society of Australian Genealogists for reading a draft of this book and giving us invaluable notes and encouragement.

To Cassie's mum, Barbara Hall, for being an extra set of eyes and sighting a typo at 10 paces away. And to our families and friends for the encouragement you gave us.

To the dedicated librarians and archivists around the country for sharing with us your insider knowledge and advice.

And to family historians everywhere – both new and experienced, amateur and professional. Your stories and research are what fires our imagination.

A big, big thank you from us,
Cassie and Shaun

Index